W9-AEK-782

Scrap Lap Quilts™

LEISURE ARTS®

Contents

Mystic Gems...4

Color Splash 10

Scrap Log Cabin 16

Autumn Evening 22

Gradations...28

Beach Birds 34

Scrap Fan Blades 42

Bejeweled 48

Twelve Crowns.......................................54

Northern Lights......................................60

Windmill Quilt..66

Amish Hearts 72

Shangri-La Quilt.....................................78

Amish Wedding Ring..............................84

Don't Put All Your Eggs in One Basket...90

Butterflies & Blossoms 100

Amish Mosaic...106

Windmill Scrappy Fun 113

General Instructions 117

SCRAP LAP QUILTS ©2003, 2001, 2000, 1999, 1998, 1997 House of White Birches, 306 East Parr Road, Berne, IN 46711, (260) 589-4000. Customer_Service @ whitebirches.com. Made in USA.

ISBN: 1-57486-344-4

CREDITS: Windmill Quilt, page 66, provided by Coats & Clark.

Introduction

If you love the idea of making a quilt but feel that a full-size bed quilt is too big a project, a lap quilt may be the perfect choice for you. Smaller than a bed quilt, a lap quilt can have many faces. It is a perfect cover on a cold winter afternoon for that short Sunday nap on the couch, or you can hang it on a wall to add warmth to your decor.

If you have been sewing for a long time, you probably have left-over scraps from other projects, or you may have acquired small bits of fabric saved for that "someday" project. A scrap lap quilt perfectly combines your desire to create a small quilt and your need to find a spot for your homeless scraps.

With just a yard of black fabric and ¼ yard scraps of yellow/gold, orange/red, blue/green and purple fabrics you can create the charming Color Splash quilt on page 10.

If you love the beach, scraps of many different colored fabrics in prints and solids along with 2 yards of a blue print will produce a wonderful memo of the beach by following the instructions for Beach Birds on page 34.

If you are more of a traditionalist, try making the scrap version of Scrap Log Cabin on page 16. A wide variety of fabrics in various hues will give you a new look for an old favorite.

After you've tried a few of these quilts, you are sure to agree that nothing could be more fun than scrap laps. ❖

Mystic Gems

BY LUCY A. FAZELY

More than 10 different fabrics are used to create this lovely quilt. If you use a mixture of bright prints and pastels, the reults will be a gem. While the multitude of pieces may make the quilt look difficult, the strip-piecing method actually makes it easy.

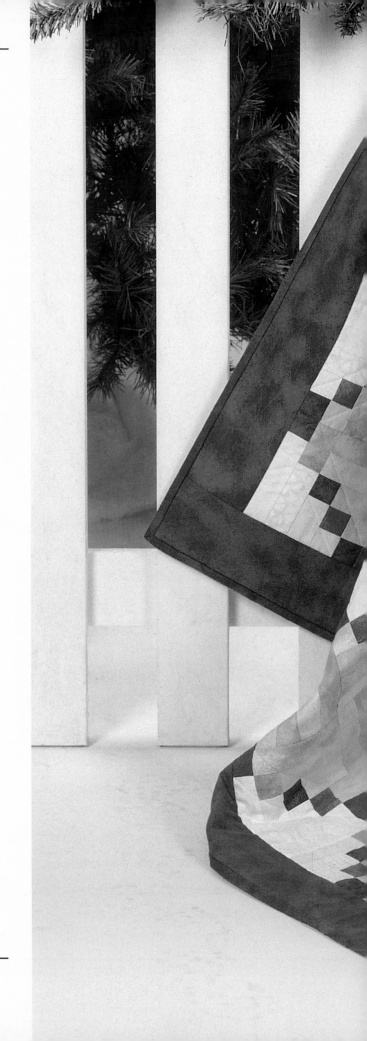

Mystic Gems

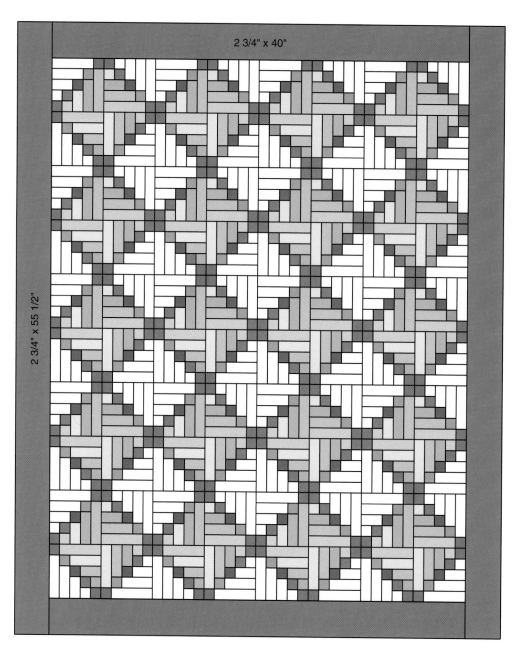

2 3/4" x 40"

2 3/4" x 55 1/2"

Mystic Gems
Placement Diagram
45 1/2" x 55 1/2"

Mystic Gems

PROJECT SPECIFICATIONS

Quilt Size: 45½" x 55½"

Block Size: 10" x 10"

Number of Blocks: 20

FABRIC & BATTING

- ¼ yard each red, green and orange prints
- 6–7 pastel-colored fabrics equivalent to 1½ yards
- Assorted white-on-white prints equivalent to 1½ yards
- 1 yard blue mottled
- Backing 50" x 60"
- Batting 50" x 60"
- 6 yards self-made or purchased binding

SUPPLIES & TOOLS

- Neutral color all-purpose thread
- Basic sewing tools and supplies, rotary cutter, mat and ruler

INSTRUCTIONS

1. Cut eight strips blue mottled 1½" by fabric width.

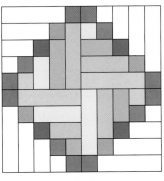

Mystic Gems
10" x 10" Block

2. Cut four strips each 1½", 2½", 3½" and 4½" by fabric width white-on-white prints.

3. Cut four strips each red, green and orange prints 1½" by width of fabric.

4. Cut a total of 30 strips 1½" by fabric width from the pastel fabrics.

5. Sew a 1½"-wide blue mottled strip to a 1½"-wide pastel strip; repeat for four different blue/pastel strip sets. *Note: Chose four different pastel fabrics at random.*

6. Sew a blue strip to each of the four 4½"-wide white-on-white print strips.

Mystic Gems

7. Sew each of the 1½"-wide red strips to the four 1½"-wide white-on-white print strips. Sew the 1½"-wide green strips to each of the 2½"-wide white-on-white print strips. Sew the 1½"-wide orange strips to each of the 3½"-wide white-on-white print strips. Press all seams toward the white-on-white print strips.

8. Cut twenty 1½" segments from each strip set referring to Figure 1.

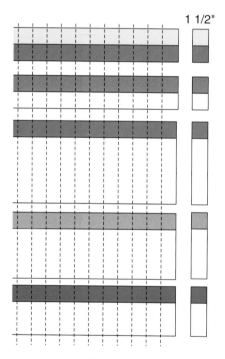

Figure 1
Cut 1 1/2" segments from strip sets.

9. To make one block unit, join a blue/pastel segment with a red/white segment to make a Four-Patch as shown in Figure 2; repeat for 80 units.

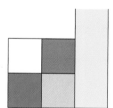

Figure 2
Join segments to make a Four-Patch as shown.

10. Sew a 1½" pastel strip to one side of a Four-Patch unit as shown in Figure 3. Trim excess strip from square as shown in Figure 4; press seam toward strip.

Figure 3
Sew a 1 1/2" pastel strip to 1 side of a Four-Patch unit.

Figure 4
Trim excess strip from square.

11. Stitch a green/white segment to the unit stitched in step 10 as shown in Figure 5.

Figure 5
Stitch a green/white segment to the stitched unit.

12. Continue adding pastel strips and segments until block unit is completed as shown in Figure 6. Join four units to complete one Mystic Gems block as shown in Figure 7; repeat to make 20 blocks.

Figure 6
Add pastel strips and segments until block unit is completed.

13. Lay out blocks in five rows of four blocks each, referring to the Placement Diagram for arrangement of blocks; press seams in one direction.

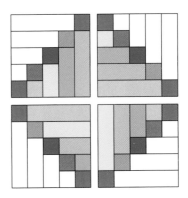

Figure 7
Join 4 units to complete 1 Mystic Gems block.

14. Cut and piece two strips each 3¼" x 40½" and 3¼" x 56" blue mottled. Sew the shorter strips to the top and bottom and the longer strips to opposite long sides of the pieced center; press seams toward strips.

15. Sandwich batting between completed top and prepared backing piece. Pin or baste layers together to hold flat.

16. Quilt as desired by hand or machine. When quilting is complete, trim edges even and remove pins or basting.

17. Bind edges with self-made or purchased binding to finish. ❖

Color Splash

BY LUCY A. FAZELY

Bright jewel-tone colors in yellow/gold, orange/red, blue/green and purple mix with black solid fabric to create a fascinating Amish-style quilt. You may want to hang this quilt on your wall as a beautiful work of art.

Color Splash

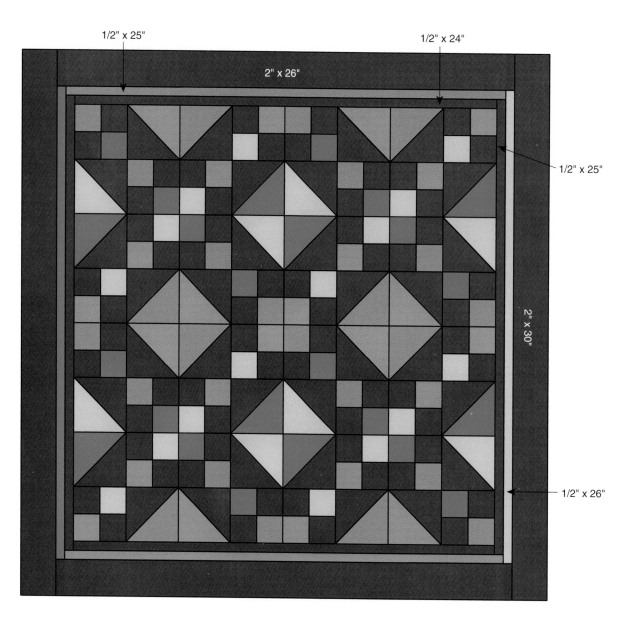

Color Splash
Placement Diagram
30" x 30"

Color Splash

PROJECT SPECIFICATIONS

Quilt Size: 30" x 30"

Block Size: 6" x 6"

Number of Blocks: 16

FABRIC & BATTING

- ¼ yard each yellow/gold, orange/red, blue/green and purple
- 1 yard black solid
- 1 yard backing fabric
- Batting 34" x 34"
- 3¾ yards self-made or purchased binding

SUPPLIES & TOOLS

- Neutral color all-purpose thread
- Clear nylon monofilament
- Basic sewing tools and supplies, rotary cutter, self-healing mat and 6½" x 24" clear ruler

INSTRUCTIONS

1. Cut one strip each yellow/gold, orange/red, blue/green and purple fabrics 3½" x 44". Cut each strip into eight 3½" segments to make squares for A. Cut three strips black solid 3½" x 44", cutting strips into 3½" segments to make 32 squares for A.

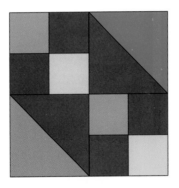

Block A
6" x 6" Block

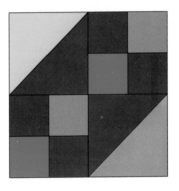

Block B
6" x 6" Block

2. Draw a diagonal line from one corner to the other corner on the wrong side of each colored A square as shown in Figure 1.

Figure 1
Draw diagonal line
on colored squares.

Color Splash

3. Place a colored A square on a black solid A square with right sides together. Stitch along marked line; trim excess fabric layers to a ¼" seam allowance as shown in Figure 2; press seams toward black solid A squares; repeat for 32 A units. Set aside.

Figure 2
Trim excess to a 1/4"
seam allowance.

4. Cut one strip each yellow/gold, orange/red, blue/green and purple fabrics and four strips black solid 2" x 44".

5. Sew a black solid strip to each of the colored strips along length with right sides together; press seams toward black solid. Cut each strip set into 2" segments to make B units; you will need 16 B units of each color.

6. Sew a yellow/black B unit to an orange/black B unit to make a Four-Patch unit as shown in Figure 3; repeat for 16 units. Sew a blue/black B unit to a purple/black B unit to make a Four-Patch unit again referring to Figure 3; repeat for 16 units.

Make 32   Make 32

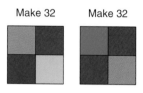

Figure 3
Join 2 B units as shown.

7. Join two orange/yellow/black Four-Patch units with one purple/black A unit and one blue/black A unit to make one A Block as shown in Figure 4; repeat for eight A Blocks.

Figure 4
Join units as shown to
make 1 A Block

8. Join two blue/purple/black Four-Patch units with one yellow/black A unit and one orange/black A unit to make one B Block as shown in Figure 5; repeat for eight B Blocks.

Figure 5
Join units as shown
to make 1 B Block

9. Join two A and two B Blocks to make a row as shown in Figure 6; repeat for two rows. Press seams in one direction.

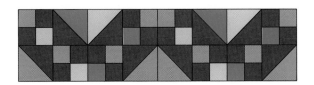

Figure 6
Arrange 2 A Blocks with 2 B Blocks to make a row.

10. Join two A and two B Blocks to make a row as shown in Figure 7; repeat for two rows. Press seams in one direction.

Figure 7
Arrange 2 A Blocks with 2 B Blocks to make a row.

11. Join rows, alternating row placement referring to the Placement Diagram; press seams in one direction.

12. Cut two strips each black solid 1" x 24½" and 1" x 25½". Sew shorter strips to top and bottom and longer strips to opposite sides; press seams toward strips.

13. Cut one strip each 1" x 25½" purple and orange/red and one strip each 1" x 26½" yellow/gold and blue/green. Sew purple strip to top and orange/red strip to bottom and blue/green and yellow/gold strips to sides referring to the Placement Diagram. Press seams toward strips.

14. Cut two strips each black solid 2½" x 26½" and 2½" x 30½". Sew shorter strips to top and bottom and longer strips to opposite sides; press seams toward strips.

15. Cut a piece of backing fabric 34" x 34". Sandwich batting between completed top and prepared backing; pin or baste layers together to hold flat.

16. Quilt as desired by hand or machine. *Note: The quilt shown was machine-quilted using clear nylon monofilament in the top of the machine and all-purpose thread to match backing in the bobbin.*

17. When quilting is complete, trim edges even. Bind with self-made or purchased binding to finish. *Note: A sleeve may be made using leftover backing fabric and added to the top backside for hanging.* ❖

Scrap Log Cabin

BY LUCY A. FAZELY

One of the most popular quilts ever made is the Log Cabin, and here it is in a new guise, a Scrap Log Cabin. If you want the quilt to have an antique look, select muted rather than bright fabrics. Instead of white backgrounds, choose tans and beiges. Select a wide variety of colors including browns, reds, greens, golds, blues and purples. Sort the fabrics from the lightest to the darkest. Medium fabrics may prove tricky as they will need to be sorted into either the dark or light piles, but they will keep the quilt from looking static.

Scrap Log Cabin

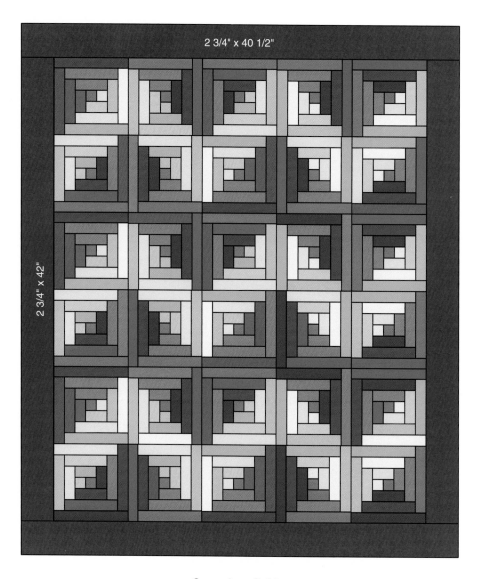

2 3/4" x 40 1/2"

2 3/4" x 42"

Scrap Log Cabin
Placement Diagram
40 1/2" x 47 1/2"

Scrap Log Cabin

PROJECT SPECIFICATIONS

Quilt Size: 40½" x 47½"

Block Size: 7" x 7"

Number of Blocks: 30

FABRIC & BATTING

- ⅛ yard dark red print
- 24 strips 1½" by fabric width of light-to-medium prints or scraps to total 1¼ yards
- 30 strips 1½" by fabric width of medium-to-dark prints or scraps to total 1½ yards
- ½ yard black print
- Backing 45" x 52"
- Batting 45" x 52"
- 5½ yards self-made or purchased binding

SUPPLIES & TOOLS

- Neutral color all-purpose thread
- Basic sewing tools and supplies, rotary cutter, mat and ruler

INSTRUCTIONS

1. Sort fabric strips in piles of light and dark.

2. Cut two strips dark red print 1½" by fabric width.

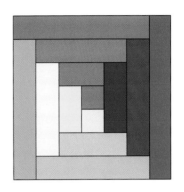

Scrap Log Cabin
7" x 7" Block

3. Cut a 10" segment from eight different light print strips. Sew these strips to two 1½"-wide dark red print strips as shown in Figure 1; press seams toward dark red print.

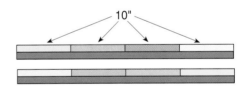

Figure 1
Sew the 10" lengths light print
to red print strips as shown.

4. Cut strip sets into 1½" segments as shown in Figure 2; you will need 30 segments. *Note: If using small scraps instead of fabric-width strips, use these for the shorter rounds in the blocks.*

5. Sew the segments to light print strips as in

Scrap Log Cabin

step 3; cut into segments using light print/dark red segments as a guide as shown in Figure 3.

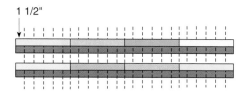

Figure 2
Cut into 1 1/2" segments as shown.

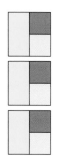

Figure 3
Sew the segments
to light print strips;
cut into segments
as shown.

6. Sew the segments to dark strips as in step 3; cut into segments as shown in Figure 4.

7. Continue sewing segments to light and dark strips, keeping dark strips on dark side of center and light strips on light side of center and pressing

seams toward newly added strips until there are three strips on each side of the center dark red print square.

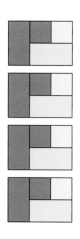

Figure 4
Cut into segments
as shown.

8. Arrange blocks in six rows of five blocks each, referring to the Placement Diagram for positioning of blocks.

9. Join blocks in rows; join rows to complete the pieced center. Press seams in one direction.

10. Cut two strips each black print 3¼" x 41" and 3¼" x 42½". Sew the longer strips to opposite long

sides and shorter strips to the top and bottom; press seams toward strips.

11. Sandwich batting between completed top and prepared backing piece. Pin or baste layers together to hold flat.

12. Quilt as desired by hand or machine. When quilting is complete, remove pins or basting; trim edges even.

13. Bind edges with self-made or purchased binding to finish. ❖

Autumn Evening

BY JUDITH SANDSTROM

The falling leaves on this quilt bring to mind those crisp autumn evenings when leaves sail to the ground in the cool breeze. These leaves are created in gold, rose, green and blue prints, just as the autumn leaves are created in many colors. If you follow the Placement Diagram carefully, your leaves will fall to the ground just as they do in nature.

Autumn Evening

3/4" x 42"

1 1/2" x 42"

Autumn Evening
Placement Diagram
33 1/2" x 47"

Autumn Evening

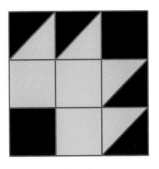

Leaf
5 1/4" x 5 1/4" Block

PROJECT SPECIFICATIONS

Quilt Size: 33½" x 47"

Block Size: 5¼" x 5¼"

Number of Blocks: 24

FABRIC & BATTING

- ⅜ yard each gold, rose, green and blue prints
- 1¼ yards black print
- Backing 38" x 51"
- Batting 38" x 51"
- 4¾ yards self-made or purchased binding

SUPPLIES & TOOLS

- Neutral color all-purpose thread
- Cream quilting thread
- Basic sewing tools and supplies, rotary cutter, mat and ruler

INSTRUCTIONS

1. Cut nine strips black print 2" by fabric width; cut four strips into 5¾" segments to make 28 sashing strips. Set aside the remaining five strips.

2. Cut three strips black print 2¼" by fabric width; subcut into 2¼" square segments for A squares. You will need 52 A squares.

3. Cut six strips black print 2⅝" by fabric width; subcut into 2⅝" square segments. Cut each square in half on one diagonal to make B triangles; you will need 178 black print B triangles.

4. Cut one strip each gold, rose, green and blue prints 2¼" by fabric width; subcut into 2¼" square segments for A. You will need 18 A squares of each color.

5. Cut two strips each gold, rose, green and blue prints 2⅝" by fabric width; subcut into 2⅝" square segments. Cut each square in half on one diagonal to make B triangles; you will need 46 B triangles of each color.

Autumn Evening

6. To make one Leaf block, sew a black print B to a colored print B as shown in Figure 1; repeat for four B units of the same color.

Figure 1
Sew a black print B
to a colored print B
as shown.

7. Arrange the B units with two black print and three same-color A squares in rows referring to Figure 2. Join the units in rows; join the rows to complete one block. Repeat for six blocks of each color.

Figure 2
Arrange the B units with 2
black print and 3 same-color
A squares in rows.

8. Arrange the blocks in rows referring to Figure 3.

Figure 3
Arrange the blocks in rows.

9. Join seven 2" x 5¾" sashing strips and six blocks to make a vertical row as shown in Figure 4. Repeat for four vertical rows; press seams in one direction.

2" x 5 3/4"

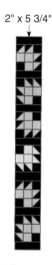

Figure 4
Join seven 2" x 5 3/4" sashing
strips and 6 blocks to make a
vertical row.

10. Cut the remaining 2" by fabric width black print strips cut in step 1 to 42½" lengths. Join the vertical rows with the strips beginning and ending with strips; press seams toward strips.

11. Cut one strip each 1¼" x 42½" gold and green prints; sew to opposite long sides of the pieced center. Press seams toward strips.

12. Sew remaining black print B triangles to remaining colored print B triangles to make triangle/square units for borders.

13. Join one B unit of each color as shown in Figure 5; repeat for 20 units.

Figure 5
Join 1 B unit of each color.

14. Join six units to complete one side border strip as shown in Figure 6; repeat for two strips. Sew a strip to opposite sides of the pieced center; press seams toward colored print strips.

Figure 6
Join 6 units to complete
1 side border strip.

15. Cut one strip each 1¼" x 34" blue and rose prints. Sew to the top and bottom of the pieced center; press seams toward strips.

16. Join four B units as shown in Figure 7; add one B unit to one end and a black print A square to both ends to complete top and bottom border strips. Sew to the pieced center; press seams toward colored print strips.

Figure 7
Join units with 1 B unit and 2 black
print A squares as shown.

17. Sandwich batting between completed top and prepared backing; pin or baste to hold.

18. Quilt as desired by hand or machine. *Note: The quilt shown was hand-quilted ¼" from seams using cream quilting thread.*

19. Remove pins or basting. Trim edges even with quilted top. Bind edges with self-made or purchased binding to finish. ❖

Gradations

BY LUCY A. FAZELY

The designer of this quilt discovered a print fabric that has light, medium and dark values of the same color on one fabric. She was able to create this quilt by choosing 13 of those prints and combining them with a black-on-black print. If you can't find a gradated print fabric, this quilt can still be made by choosing light, medium and dark fabrics in the same color family for your gradations.

Gradations

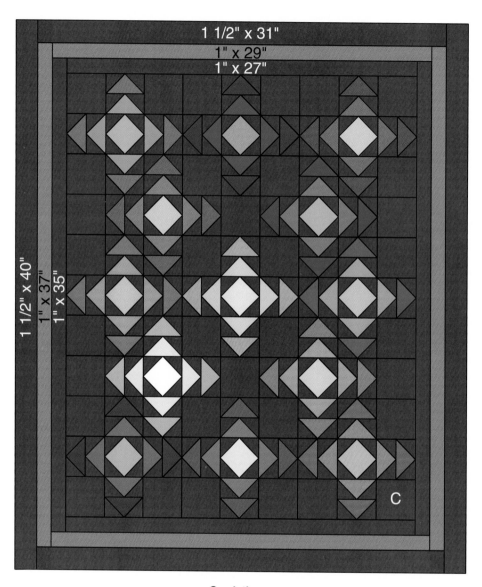

Gradations
Placement Diagram
34" x 40"

Gradations

PROJECT SPECIFICATIONS

Quilt Size: 34" x 40"

FABRIC & BATTING

- ⅛ yard each of 12 gradational prints (print has light, medium and dark values of the same color on one fabric)
- ⅓ yard of 1 gradational print
- 1¾ yards black-on-black print
- Backing 38" x 44"
- Batting 38" x 44"
- 4¼ yards self-made or purchased black binding

SUPPLIES & TOOLS

- Neutral color all-purpose thread
- White or yellow fabric marker
- Basic sewing tools and supplies, rotary cutter, mat and ruler

INSTRUCTIONS

1. From each of the 13 gradational prints cut the following: one 3½" x 3½" square lightest part of fabric for A; four 2" x 3½" rectangles medium part of fabric for B; and four 2" x 3½" rectangles darkest part of fabric for B.

2. Cut three strips black-on-black print 3½" by fabric width; subcut strips into 3½" square segments for C. You will need 34 C squares.

3. Cut 13 strips black-on-black print 2" by fabric width; subcut strips into 2" square segments for D. You will need 260 D squares.

4. Using a white or yellow fabric maker, draw a diagonal line on the wrong side of each black-on-black print D square.

5. To make one block, lay a D square right sides together on an A square corner as shown in Figure 1; stitch on drawn line.

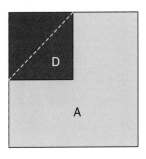

Figure 1
Stitch along marked line.

Gradations

6. Trim excess beyond stitched line to ¼" as shown in Figure 2; press up to make a triangle on the corner of A. Repeat on all corners of A to complete an A-D unit as shown in Figure 3. Press seams toward D.

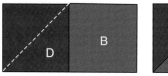

Figure 4
Sew D to short sides of B.

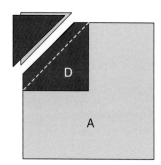

Figure 2
Cut 1/4" beyond stitched line.

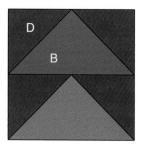

Figure 5
Join 2 D-B-D units as shown.

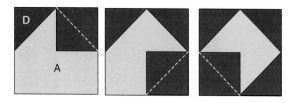

Figure 3
Repeat on all corners of A.

7. Sew a D square to each short side of the medium and dark B rectangles using the same method as in steps 5 and 6 referring to Figure 4 to complete Flying Geese units.

8. Join a medium and dark Flying Geese unit as shown in Figure 5; repeat for four units. Set all pieces aside.

9. Repeat steps 5–8 to complete 13 different-colored sets of block units.

10. Lay out all the completed units in rows with C squares as shown in Figure 6. *Note: The pieces cannot be stitched together to make blocks because the blocks are interconnected.*

11. Join units in rows; join rows to complete pieced center. Press seams in one direction.

12. Cut two strips each 1½" x 27½" and 1½" x 35½" black-on-black print. Sew the shorter strips to opposite short sides and longer strips to opposite long sides; press seams toward strips.

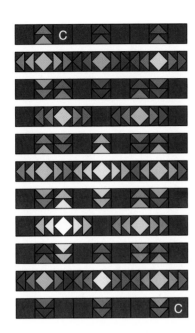

Figure 6
Lay out pieced units with C in rows.

13. Cut two strips each 1½" x 29½" and 1½" x 37½" from the ⅓ yard gradational fabric. Sew shorter strips to top and bottom and longer strips to opposite long sides; press seams toward strips.

14. Cut two strips each 2" x 31½" and 2" x 40½" black-on-black print. Sew shorter strips to opposite short sides and longer strips to opposite long sides; press seams toward strips.

15. Sandwich batting between completed top and prepared backing piece; pin or baste layers together to hold.

16. Quilt as desired by hand or machine.

17. When quilting is complete, remove pins or basting, trim edges even and bind with self-made or purchased black binding to finish. ❖

Beach Birds

BY JUDITH SANDSTROM

A variety of birds in all sizes hover at the beach and make the perfect subjects for a quilt for beach lovers. All of the large birds use the same fabric for their legs as do the small birds. The medium-size birds may have two different leg fabrics if desired. All of the Bird blocks are pieced in the same manner. The pattern pieces are labeled with letters and numbers. The letters are the same for each block; the numbers indicate the different sizes. A1 indicates that the pattern is for the 6" block, A2 for the 9" block and A3 for the 12" block.

Beach Birds

Beach Birds
Placement Diagram
42" x 54"

Beach Birds

Project Specifications

Quilt Size: 42" x 54"

Block Size: 6" x 6", 9" x 9" and 12" x 12"

Number of Blocks: 12 each small and medium, and 6 large

Fabrics & Batting

- ⅛ yard each or scraps of three different beak fabrics in black, light gold and dark gold
- ¼ yard each or scraps of 3 or 4 different leg fabrics in dark tan, light tan, black or brown
- ⅓ yard each or scraps of several different body fabrics in gray, tan, brown or black prints
- 2 yards blue print for background
- Backing 46" x 58"
- Batting 46" x 58"
- 5¾ yards self-made or purchased binding

Supplies & Tools

- Neutral color all-purpose thread
- White hand-quilting thread
- Basic sewing supplies and tools, rotary cutter, mat and ruler

Instructions

1. Prepare templates using pattern pieces given; cut as directed on each piece.

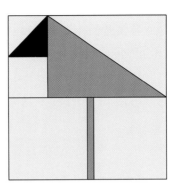

Beach Bird
6" x 6", 9" x 9" and 12" x 12" Blocks

2. To piece one of any size block, sew a light blue print A to a beak fabric A along the diagonal. Add B to the dark side as shown in Figure 1.

Figure 1
Sew a light blue print A to a beak fabric A along the diagonal. Add B to the dark side as shown.

3. Sew a blue print C to a body fabric print C along the diagonal.

4. Sew the C unit to the A-B unit to complete the head/body section of the block as shown in Figure 2.

Figure 2
Sew the C unit to the A-B unit to complete the head/body section of the block.

5. Sew E between D and F to complete the leg section of the block as shown in Figure 3.

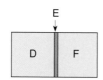

Figure 3
Sew E between D and F
to complete the leg
section of the block.

6. Join the head/body section with the leg section to complete one block; repeat for six large and 12 each small and medium blocks.

7. Join two small blocks as shown in Figure 4; repeat for six two-block units.

Figure 4
Join 2 small blocks
as shown.

8. Arrange the two-block units with the medium and large blocks to make sections as shown in Figure 5. Join the units as arranged; press seams in one direction.

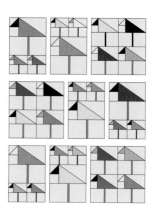

Figure 5
Arrange the 2-block units with
the medium and large blocks to
make sections as shown.

9. Join the pieced sections to complete the pieced top.

10. Sandwich batting between completed top and prepared backing; pin or baste layers together to hold flat.

11. Quilt as desired by hand or machine. *Note: The quilt shown was hand-quilted with white quilting thread ¼" away from seams around bird shapes.*

12. When quilting is complete, trim edges even and remove pins or basting. Bind edges with self-made or purchased binding to finish. ❖

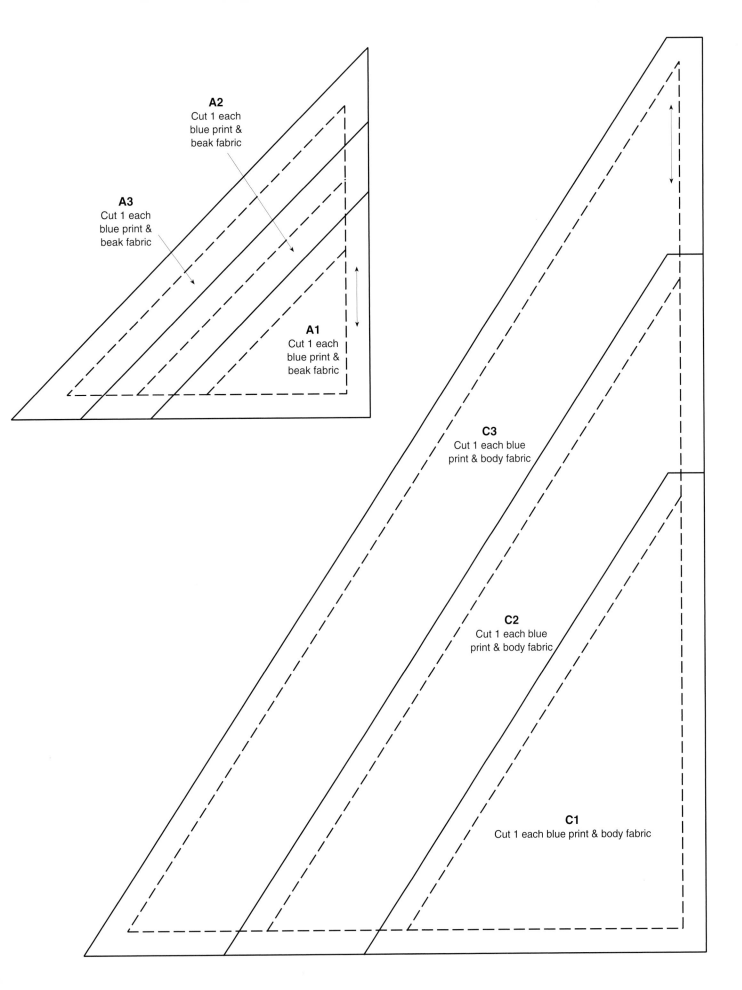

A2
Cut 1 each
blue print &
beak fabric

A3
Cut 1 each
blue print &
beak fabric

A1
Cut 1 each
blue print &
beak fabric

C3
Cut 1 each blue
print & body fabric

C2
Cut 1 each blue
print & body fabric

C1
Cut 1 each blue print & body fabric

Beach Birds

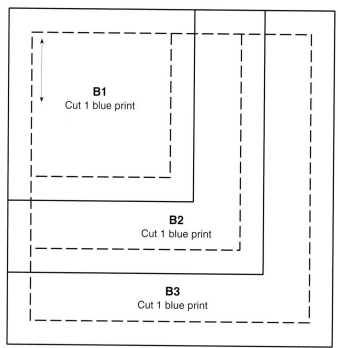

B1
Cut 1 blue print

B2
Cut 1 blue print

B3
Cut 1 blue print

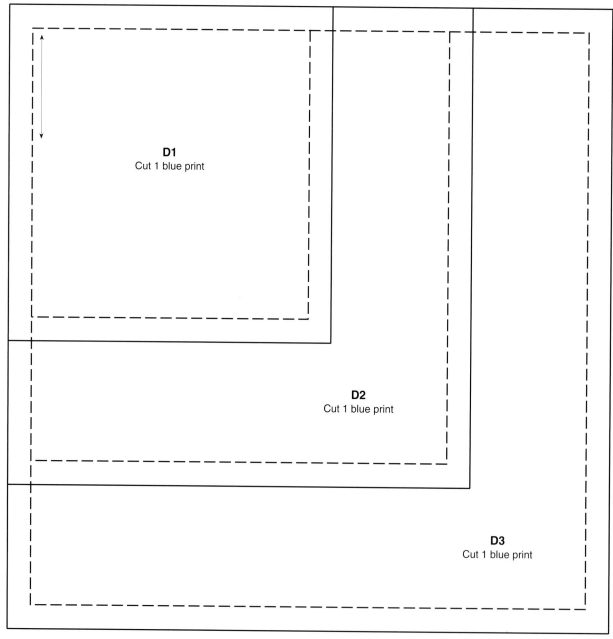

D1
Cut 1 blue print

D2
Cut 1 blue print

D3
Cut 1 blue print

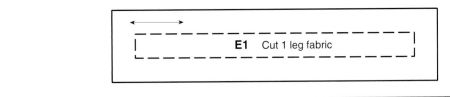

E1 Cut 1 leg fabric

E2 Cut 1 leg fabic

E3
Cut 1 leg fabric

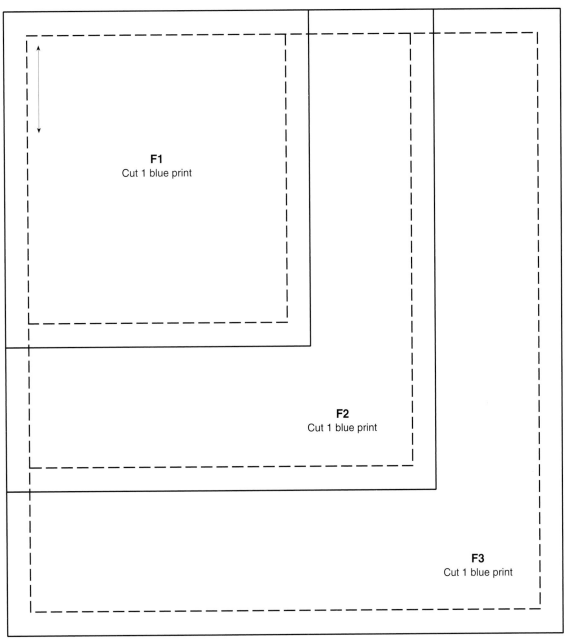

F1
Cut 1 blue print

F2
Cut 1 blue print

F3
Cut 1 blue print

Scrap Fan Blades

BY LUCY A. FAZELY

Fan Blades is one of those quilt designs that resembles its name. If the block could rotate, you'd feel the breezes. With a basket of scraps in light, medium and dark fabrics, and a leisurely day, you could probably sew this neat little quilt in just one day. It's a great pattern for a beginning quilter because it is easy and fun, and the results are so lovely.

Scrap Fan Blades

Scrap Fan Blades
Placement Diagram
36" x 36"

Scrap Fan Blades

PROJECT SPECIFICATIONS

Wall Quilt Size: 36" x 36"

Block Size: 6" x 6"

Number of Blocks: 25

FABRIC & BATTING

- ¼ yard total medium print scraps
- ⅔ yard total light print scraps
- 1 yard total dark print scraps
- Backing 40" x 40"
- Batting 40" x 40"
- 4¼ yards self-made or purchased binding

SUPPLIES & TOOLS

- Neutral color all-purpose thread
- Basic sewing supplies and tools

INSTRUCTIONS

Note: Use ¼" seam allowance throughout. Press seams to one side.

1. Cut scraps into 2" x 3½" rectangles as follows: 40 medium print, 60 dark print and 100 light print.

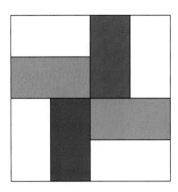

Fan Blade
6" x 6" Block

2. Sew a light print rectangle to each of the medium and dark print rectangles as shown in Figure 1; press seams away from the light print rectangles.

Figure 1
Sew a light 2" x 3 1/2" rectangle to
a dark 2" x 3 1/2" rectangle.

3. Make nine blocks using all dark fan blades referring to Figure 2. Make four blocks with all medium fan blades, referring to Figure 3. Make 12 blocks with medium and dark fan blades alternating referring to Figure 4.

Scrap Fan Blades

Figure 2
Make 9 blocks using dark fan blades.

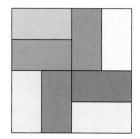

Figure 3
Make 4 blocks using
medium fan blades.

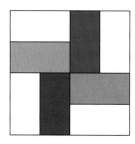

Figure 4
Make 12 blocks combining
medium and dark fan blades.

4. Arrange blocks in rows referring to the Placement Diagram for positioning of blocks. Join blocks in rows; join rows to complete pieced center. Press seams in one direction.

5. Cut remaining dark scraps into 88 rectangles 2" x 3½". Stitch these rectangles into 44 border blocks as shown in Figure 5.

Figure 5
Make 1 border block;
repeat for 44 blocks.

6. Make two border strips using 10 alternating blocks as shown in Figure 6. Make two border strips using 12 alternating blocks.

Figure 6
Join 10 border blocks to make a strip as shown.

7. Sew the 10-block border strips to two opposite sides referring to the Placement Diagram for positioning. Sew the 12-unit border strips to the remaining sides, again referring to the Placement Diagram for positioning.

8. Sandwich batting between completed top and prepared backing piece; pin or baste layers together.

9. Hand- or machine-quilt in the ditch of seams and as desired.

10. When quilting is complete, remove pins or basting. Bind edges with self-made or purchased binding to finish. ❖

Bejeweled

BY LUCY A. FAZELY

While this pattern will work very well with a collection of scraps, the photographed quilt was actually made with a coordinated collection from one manufacturer. The quilt is made with nine fat quarters of dark/medium prints and nine fat quarters of light/medium prints along with extra fabric for the borders. While the pattern is simple and easy to follow, the results are wonderful.

Bejeweled

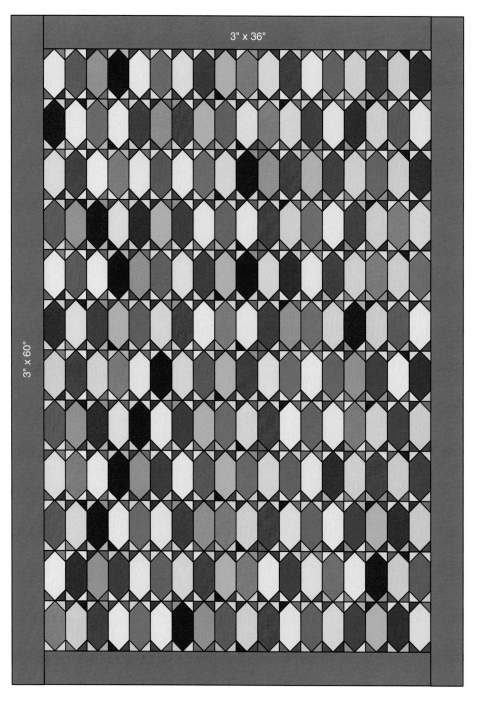

Bejeweled
Placement Diagram
42" x 60"

Bejeweled

PROJECT SPECIFICATIONS

Quilt Size: 42" x 60"

Block Size: 2" x 4½"

Number of Blocks: 216

FABRIC & BATTING

- 9 fat quarters dark/medium prints
- 9 fat quarters light/medium prints
- ⅝ yard purple print
- Backing 46" x 64"
- Batting 46" x 64"
- 6 yards self-made or purchased binding

SUPPLIES & TOOLS

- Neutral color all-purpose thread
- Clear nylon monofilament
- Basic sewing tools and supplies, rotary cutter, mat and ruler

INSTRUCTIONS

1. Cut two strips each dark/medium and light/medium prints 5" x 18". Subcut strips into 2½" segments for A. You will need 12 A rectangles from each print.

Bejeweled
2" x 4 1/2" Block

2. Cut four strips each dark/medium and light/medium prints 1½" x 18". Subcut strips into 1½" segments for B. You will need 48 B squares from each print.

3. Draw a diagonal line on the wrong side of each B square as shown in Figure 1.

Figure 1
Draw a diagonal line
on the wrong side of
each B square.

4. Randomly choose four light/medium B squares and a dark/medium A rectangle.

Bejeweled

5. Place one B square on one corner of A placing the diagonal line as shown in Figure 2; sew on the marked line.

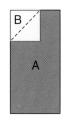

Figure 2
Place 1 B square on 1 corner of A placing the diagonal line as shown.

6. Repeat with a second B square on opposite end corner as shown in Figure 3; press B pieces to right side as shown in Figure 4. *Note: You may trim seam allowance to ¼" as shown in Figure 5 or leave the double layer of fabric to stabilize the units.*

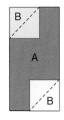

Figure 3
Repeat with a second B square on opposite end corner as shown.

Figure 4
Press B pieces to right side as shown.

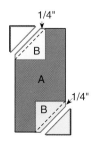

Figure 5
Trim seam allowance to 1/4" as shown.

7. Pin and sew remaining B squares to remaining corners of A; press to complete one unit as shown in Figure 6. Repeat for all light/medium B squares and dark/medium A rectangles, and dark/medium B squares and light/medium A rectangles.

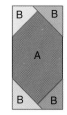

Figure 6
Press B pieces to the right side to complete 1 block.

8. Lay out blocks in 12 rows of 18 blocks each alternating light and dark blocks referring to the Placement Diagram.

9. Join blocks in rows; join rows to complete pieced center. Press seams in one direction.

10. Cut (and piece as necessary) two strips each purple print 3½" x 36½" and 3½" x 60½". Sew the shorter strips to the short sides of the pieced center and longer strips to opposite long sides; press seams toward strips.

11. Sandwich batting between completed top and prepared backing piece; pin or baste layers together to hold flat.

12. Quilt as desired by hand or machine. *Note: The quilt shown was machine-quilted in the ditch of seams using clear nylon monofilament in the top of the machine and all-purpose thread in the bobbin. The border was quilted in straight lines with 1", ¼", ¾" and ¼" spacing.*

13. When quilting is complete, trim edges even; remove pins or basting. Bind edges with self-made or purchased binding to finish. ❖

Twelve Crowns

BY LUCY A. FAZELY

A traditional quilt block, Twelve Crowns, makes an appearance here as a scrap quilt that uses coordinated prints, all of which work together to make a pretty quilt. The quilt requires 12 scraps of coordinating prints plus several yards of striped border prints. If you love prints and have scraps in your scrap stash, this is a good way to use them. You can use an allover print for the "crowns," but if you use a border print, you will need to "fussy-cut" each piece on the same section of the print to achieve the uniform look of the 12 crowns.

Twelve Crowns

6 1/2" x 49"

Twelve Crowns
Placement Diagram
49" x 49"

Twelve Crowns

Twelve Crowns
9" x 9" Block

PROJECT SPECIFICATIONS

Quilt Size: 49" x 49"

Block Size: 9" x 9"

Number of Blocks: 12

FABRIC & BATTING

- 1¼ yards tan background print
- 4" x 8" piece each 12 coordinating prints
- 1 yard striped border print 1 for piecing (if using allover print, ¼ yard is needed)
- 2 yards striped border print 2 for borders
- Backing 53" x 53"
- Batting 53" x 53"
- 5¾ yards self-made or purchased binding

SUPPLIES & TOOLS

- Neutral color all-purpose thread
- 1 spool quilting thread
- Basic sewing supplies and tools and 6½" x 24" clear ruler

INSTRUCTIONS

Note: If using a border print, you will need to fussy-cut each piece, which means each piece must be cut on the same section of the print. This adds to the yardage needed. A ¼" seam allowance is included in all measurements.

1. Cut the following from tan background: one strip 6⅞" by fabric width and cut into 6⅞" segments; one strip 9½" by fabric width and cut into 9½" segments; one strip 3½" by fabric width and cut into 3½" segments; and five strips 3⅞" by fabric width and cut into 3⅞" segments.

2. Cut two squares 3⅞" x 3⅞" from each of the 12 coordinating prints.

3. Cut each of the tan background and coordinating 3⅞" x 3⅞" squares in half on one diagonal to make triangles. Sew a tan background triangle to each of the coordinating triangles to make triangle/squares.

Twelve Crowns

4. Cut 12 triangles from striped border print 1 for pieces using A template given, carefully cutting four of the triangles identical to each other for the center blocks and eight identical to each other for the outside blocks. *Note: Use caution when cutting, handling or sewing on the bias-cut edge of these triangles.*

5. Cut each of the 6⅞" x 6⅞" tan background squares in half on one diagonal to make triangles. Sew each background triangle to a striped border print 1 triangle.

6. Join two triangle/squares as shown in Figure 1, making 12 of each combination. Sew a 3½" x 3½" tan background square to the end of half of the units as shown in Figure 2.

Make 12   Make 12

Figure 1
Join 2 triangle/squares.

Figure 2
Sew a 3 1/2" square to
1 end of 24 units.

7. Lay out the pieced units with the larger triangle/squares. Join units to make one block as shown in Figure 3. Repeat for 12 blocks. *Note: Center block uses four identical triangles.*

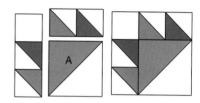

Figure 3
Arrange units to make 1 block.

8. Arrange pieced blocks with 9½" x 9½" tan background squares in four rows referring to Figure 4. Join blocks in rows; join rows to complete pieced center.

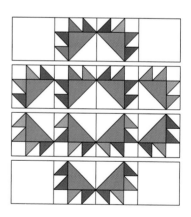

Figure 4
Arrange blocks in rows.

9. Cut four 7" x 72" strips from length of striped border print 2. *Note: Strips are cut extra long to allow*

for matching strips exactly to make a good corner turn. Excess is trimmed off after mitering. Choose an identical center point on each strip. Match the center point of each strip on sides of quilt center; pin strips in place. Starting and stopping seam ¼" from each edge of quilt, sew each border strip to sides, mitering corners; press seams toward strips. Trim excess at mitered seam after pressing.

10. Sandwich batting between completed top and prepared backing piece. Pin or baste layers to hold flat.

11. Quilt as desired by hand or machine.

12. When quilting is complete, trim edges even. Bind with self-made or purchased binding to finish. ❖

Note: *If using border stripe, place this edge on stripe pattern line.*

Note: *If using allover print, place this edge on straight of grain.*

A
Cut 4 identical striped
border print
Cut 8 identical striped
border print

Northern Lights

BY MICHELE CRAWFORD

The northern lights appear in the northern skies from time to time. Some of the fabrics used in this quilt have northern themes and feature Eskimos and polar bears. The designer was encouraged, therefore, to name her quilt *Northern Lights* because it reminded her of the northern skies. You may prefer to work with a different fabric combination. Whatever fabric you choose, this pattern will produce a beautiful quilt.

Northern Lights

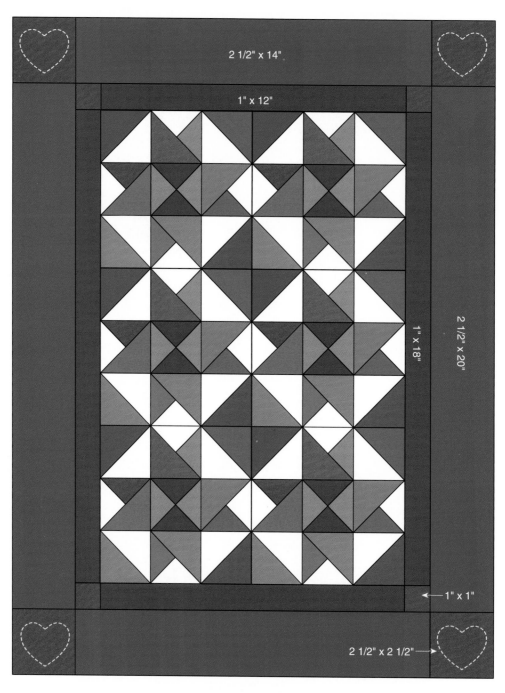

Northern Lights
Placement Diagram
19" x 25"

Northern Lights

Project Specifications

Quilt Size: 19" x 25"

Block Size: 6" x 6"

Number of Blocks: 6

Fabric & Batting

- ⅛ yard each blue, red, brown and tan with large star prints
- ⅛ yard each green, red, blue and cream solids
- ⅛ yard each blue, red, brown and green with small stars prints
- ¼ yard red-and-blue moon print
- 1 yard allover print
- Cotton batting 21" x 27"

Supplies & Tools

- 1 spool medium gray all-purpose thread
- 1 spool each light tan and cornflower blue quilting thread
- 1 package brick wide bias tape
- 4 (⅝") wood buttons
- ¼" masking tape
- Basic sewing supplies and tools, rotary cutter, mat and ruler

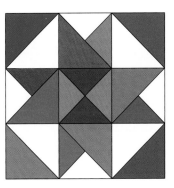

Northern Lights
6" x 6" Block

Instructions

Note: Use a ¼" seam allowance. Sew pieces with right sides together and raw edges even with matching thread. Press seam allowance toward darkest fabric.

1. Cut 2⅞" x 2⅞" squares from the following fabrics: three blue with large stars for B; three red with large stars for R; 12 solid cream for C; three solid green for G; three solid blue for BL; three green with small stars for GS; three red with small stars for RS; and six brown with small stars for BS. Cut each square in half on one diagonal to make triangles.

2. Cut 2¼" x 2¼" squares from the following fabrics: six red-and-blue moon print for M; 12

Northern Lights

tan with large stars for T; nine brown with large stars for BR; three solid red for SR; three green with large stars for SG; and three blue with small stars for SB. Cut each square in half on one diagonal to make triangles.

3. Referring to Figure 1, join the triangles to make squares. Arrange the triangle/squares in rows; join rows to complete one block. Repeat for six blocks.

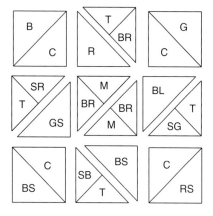

Figure 1
Join pieces in units; join units
to complete 1 block.

4. Arrange blocks in three rows of two blocks each. Join in rows; join rows to complete pieced center. Press.

5. Cut two strips red-and-blue moon print 1½" x 12½". Sew a strip to the top and bottom of the pieced center. Cut two more strips 1½" x 18½". Cut four squares red solid 1½" x 1½". Sew a square to the end of each strip. Sew these strips to opposite long sides of the pieced center.

6. Cut two strips allover print 3" x 14½"; sew to top and bottom of the pieced center. Cut two more strips 3" x 20½". Cut four squares red solid 3" x 3". Sew a square to each end of each strip. Sew these strips to the opposite long sides of the pieced center.

7. Cut a 21" x 27" piece allover print for backing. Center the batting on the wrong side of this piece. Center the wrong side of the quilt on the batting; pin or baste layers together.

8. With cornflower blue quilting thread, machine-quilt by crosshatching just the quilt center and in the seams of the blocks. Using light tan thread, hand-quilt ¼" in on each side of the frame border using masking tape as a stitching guide.

Heart Quilting Design

9. Sew a wood button in the small corner squares on borders.

10. Hand-quilt a heart in each outside border square using pattern given and cornflower blue thread.

11. Topstitch around quilt top ⅛" from edge. Trim excess backing and batting even with quilt top.

12. Sew the wide bias tape around quilt edges, mitering corners and overlapping ends. Turn bias tape to the backside of quilt; hand-stitch in place to finish. ❖

Windmill Quilt

BY MICHELE CRAWFORD

Sometimes it is hard to tell what a quilt block should be called, but there is no denying that these are windmills. You can almost see them turning in the wind. To give the project a homespun look, try using Osnaburg as the ecru background.

Windmill Quilt

Windmill Quilt
Placement Diagram
33" x 45"

Windmill Quilt

Project Specifications

Wall Quilt Size: 33" x 45"

Block Size: 12" x 12"

Number of Blocks: 6

Fabric & Batting

- ⅛ yard each tan plaid (TP), rose tiles (RT), blue leaf (BL) and brown print (BR) for border triangles
- ⅙ yard each rose plaid (R), brown leaf (BL) and blue print (B)
- ¼ yard blue plaid (BP)
- ½ yard maroon print (MP)
- 1 yard Osnaburg or ecru solid (O)
- Backing 37" x 49"
- Fleece 37" x 49"

Supplies & Tools

- 1 spool each nickel, barberry red and natural all-purpose thread
- 1 spool transparent nylon monofilament
- 1 spool natural hand-quilting thread
- 2 packages barberry red wide bias tape
- Basic sewing supplies and tools and ¼" masking tape, rotary cutter, mat and ruler

Instructions

Note: Use a ¼" seam allowance unless otherwise indicated. Sew pieces with right sides together and

Windmill Block 1
12" x 12" Block
Make 3

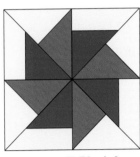

Windmill Block 2
12" x 12" Block
Make 3

raw edges even with matching thread. Press seam allowances toward darkest fabrics.

1. Cut six 5⅜" x 5⅜" squares from each of the following fabrics: rose plaid (R), blue print (B), blue plaid (BP) and maroon print (MP). Cut each square in half on one diagonal to make 12 triangles from each fabric.

2. Cut 12 squares Osnaburg 5⅜" x 5⅜". Cut each square in half on one diagonal to make 24 O triangles.

3. Prepare template for piece 1. Cut as directed on piece.

4. Sew piece 1 to a rose plaid and a blue plaid triangle to make 1R and 1BP units as shown in Figure 1; repeat for 12 of each unit.

5. Sew a blue print triangle to an Osnaburg triangle to make an O-B unit as shown in Figure 2; repeat for 12 units. Sew a maroon print triangle

Windmill Quilt

to an Osnaburg triangle, again referring to Figure 2; repeat for 12 units.

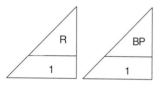

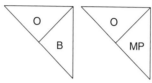

Figure 1
Make 1-R and 1-BP
units as shown.

Figure 2
Make O-B and O-MP
units as shown.

6. Sew an O-B unit to a 1-R unit as shown in Figure 3; repeat for four units. Join the units to complete Block 1 as shown in Figure 4; repeat for three blocks.

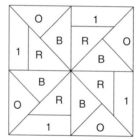

Figure 3
Sew an O-B unit to a
1-R unit as shown.

Figure 4
Join 4 units to complete
Block 1 as shown.

7. Sew an O-MP unit to a 1-BP unit; repeat for four units. Join units to complete Block 2 as shown in Figure 5; repeat for three blocks.

8. Sew Block 1 to Block 2 to make a row; repeat for three rows. Join the rows, referring to the Placement Diagram for positioning of rows; press.

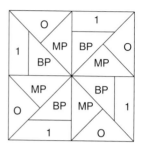

Figure 5
Join 4 units to complete
Block 2 as shown.

9. Cut two strips each brown leaf and maroon prints 1¼" x 24½" and 1¼" x 36½". Sew a 24½" brown leaf strip to a 24½" maroon print strip along length; press. Repeat with second set of strips and with the 36½" strips.

10. Cut four squares blue plaid 2" x 2". Sew a 24½" stitched strip to the top and bottom of the pieced center; press seams toward strips. Sew a blue plaid square to each end of the remaining two strips; sew these strips to opposite long sides of the pieced center; press.

11. Cut the following 3⅞" x 3⅞" squares: seven tan plaid; five each blue leaf, rose tiles and brown print; and 22 Osnaburg. Cut each square in half on one diagonal to make triangles.

12. Sew a print or plaid triangle to an Osnaburg triangle to make a triangle/square; repeat for 44 units.

13. Position the triangle/squares to make strips as shown in Figure 6. Join units to make border strips. Sew the shorter strips to the top and bottom of the pieced center. Press seams toward strips.

14. Cut four squares blue plaid 3½" x 3½". Sew a square to each end of the remaining pieced strips. Sew a strip to opposite long sides of pieced center. Press seams toward strips.

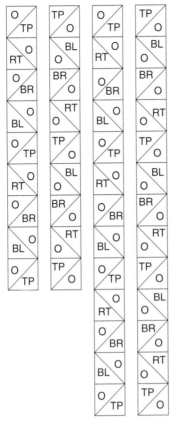

Figure 6
Position triangles as shown to make border strips.

15. Sandwich fleece between prepared backing and completed top; pin or baste layers together.

16. With natural thread in the bobbin and monofilament in the top of the machine, machine-quilt in the diagonal seams of each block, in between blocks and in the ditch of border seams. Topstitch ⅛" from edges of quilt all around.

17. Using masking tape as a stitching guide, hand-quilt using hand-quilting thread in colored triangles ¼" from two edges as shown in Figure 7.

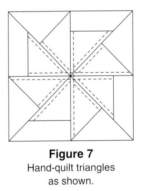

Figure 7
Hand-quilt triangles as shown.

18. When quilting is complete, remove pins or basting; trim edges even. Bind with bias tape, mitering corners and overlapping ends to finish. ❖

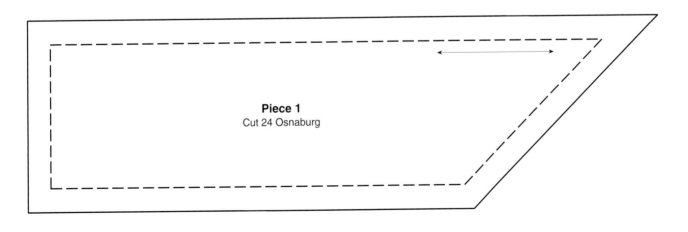

Piece 1
Cut 24 Osnaburg

Amish Hearts

BY LINDA DENNER

The hearts in this quilt are made in a most creative manner. First, four scrap squares are randomly sewn together to make a Four-Patch unit. Then a heart template is placed on the four-patch and cut out. The resulting heart is appliquéd onto a black square. The pieced hearts stand out on the black solid background giving the quilt an Amish flavor.

Amish Hearts

4" x 30"

4" x 40"

Amish Hearts
Placement Diagram
38" x 48"

Amish Hearts

Project Specifications

Quilt Size: 38" x 48"

Block Size: 10" x 10"

Number of Blocks: 12

Fabric & Batting

- 1 yard total assorted solids with a minimum of 5 colors
- 1½ yards black solid
- Backing 42" x 52"
- Batting 42" x 52"
- 5¼ yards self-made or purchased binding

Supplies & Tools

- Black all-purpose thread
- Clear nylon monofilament
- ⅜ yard fabric stabilizer
- Basic sewing tools and supplies

Instructions

1. Cut 24 squares assorted solids (excluding black) 3½" x 3½". Join four squares randomly to make a Four-Patch unit as shown in Figure 1.

2. Prepare template for heart shape using pattern given; transfer matching lines to template. Place heart template on a Four-Patch unit matching

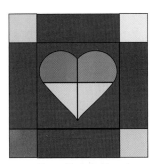

Four-Patch Heart
10" x 10" Block

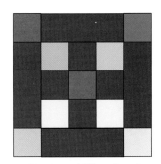

Bordered Nine-Patch
10" x 10" Block

lines as shown in Figure 2; cut out shape to make a pieced heart. Repeat for six pieced hearts.

Figure 1
Join 4 squares randomly to make a Four-Patch unit.

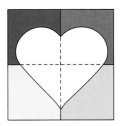

Figure 2
Place heart template on a Four-Patch unit matching lines as shown.

3. Cut one strip black solid 6½" by fabric width; subcut into 6½" segments for A. You will need six A squares.

Amish Hearts

4. Cut three strips black solid 6½" by fabric width; subcut into 2½" segments for B. You will need 48 B rectangles.

5. Cut 48 squares assorted solids 2½" x 2½" for C.

6. Sew a C square to each end of 24 B rectangles.

7. Sew B to two opposite sides of A; sew B-C to the remaining sides of A as shown in Figure 3. Repeat for six A-B-C units.

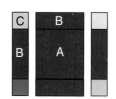

Figure 3
Sew B-C to the
remaining sides of A-B.

8. Turn under edges of a pieced heart ¼"; baste and press.

9. Center a pieced heart on the A part of the A-B-C square; pin or baste in place. Place a piece of fabric stabilizer on the wrong side of A behind heart shape.

10. Using clear nylon monofilament in the top of the machine and all-purpose thread in the bobbin, machine-appliqué heart in place using a blind-hem

stitch to complete one Four-Patch Heart block; repeat for six Four-Patch Heart blocks. Remove stabilizer.

11. Cut 30 squares assorted solids and 24 squares black solid 2½" x 2½". Join squares as shown in Figure 4 to make rows; join rows to complete one Nine-Patch unit. Repeat for six Nine-Patch units.

12. Sew B to opposite sides of each Nine-Patch unit as shown in Figure 5. Sew a B-C unit to the remaining sides to complete six Bordered Nine-Patch blocks.

Figure 4
Join squares as shown to
make rows; join rows to
complete 1 Nine-Patch unit.

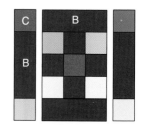

Figure 5
Sew B to opposite sides of a Nine-Patch unit.
Sew a B-C unit to the remaining sides to
complete 1 Bordered Nine-Patch block.

13. Join two Four-Patch Heart blocks with one Bordered Nine-Patch block to make a row as shown in Figure 6; repeat for two rows. Press seams in one direction.

14. Join two Bordered Nine-Patch blocks with one Four-Patch Heart block to make a row as shown in Figure 7; repeat for two rows. Press seams in one direction.

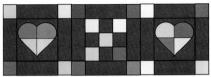

Figure 6
Join 2 Heart blocks with 1 Bordered
Nine-Patch block to make a row.

Figure 7
Join 2 Bordered Nine-Patch blocks
with 1 Heart block to make a row.

15. Join the rows to complete the pieced center referring to the Placement Diagram for positioning of rows; press seams in one direction.

16. Cut 16 squares assorted solids 2½" x 2½". Join four squares to make a Four-Patch unit, again referring to Figure 1; repeat for four Four-Patch units.

17. Cut two strips each 4½" x 40½" and 4½" x 30½" black solid. Sew the shorter strips to the top and bottom of the pieced center. Sew a Four-Patch unit to each end of the remaining two strips; sew a strip to opposite long sides of the pieced center. Press seams toward strips.

18. Sandwich batting between completed top and prepared backing piece; pin or baste layers together.

19. Quilt as desired by hand or machine. *Note: The quilt shown was machine-quilted using several different purchased patterns with clear nylon monofilament in the top of the machine and all-purpose thread in the bobbin.*

20. When quilting is complete, remove pins or basting; trim edges even. Bind with self-made or purchased binding to finish. ❖

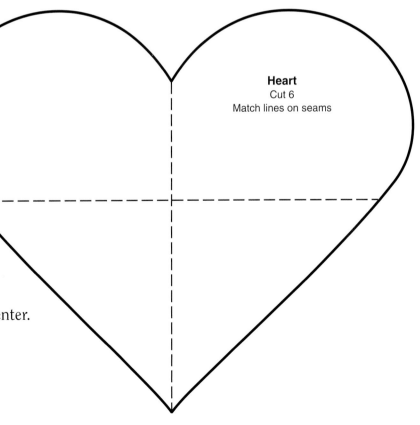

Heart
Cut 6
Match lines on seams

Shangri-La Quilt

BY MICHELE CRAWFORD

Simple quilt blocks when put together will often create interesting secondary designs. When the blocks of this quilt are joined together without any sashing, an entirely new and intriguing design is created as you can see in the photograph.

Shangri-La Quilt

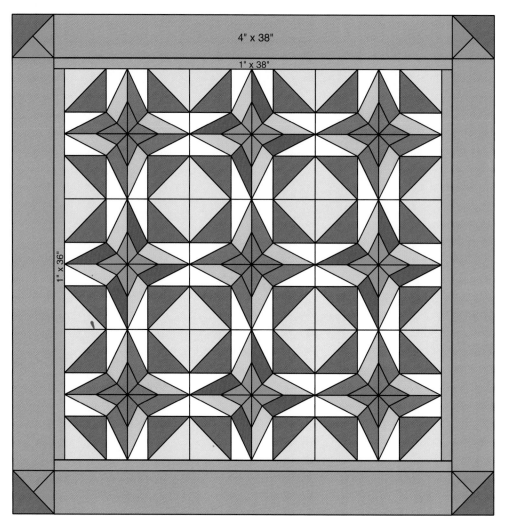

Shangri-La Quilt
Placement Diagram
46" x 46"

Shangri-La Quilt

Project Specifications

Quilt Size: 46" x 46"

Block Size: 12" x 12"

Number of Blocks: 9

Fabric & Batting

- ¼ yard light rose print
- ¼ yard each rust and green florals
- ¼ yard each rust and blue prints
- ⅓ yard each green and rose prints
- ½ yard each purple print and blue floral
- ½ yard white-on-white print
- ⅝ yard multicolored print
- Backing 50" x 50"
- Batting 50" x 50"
- 5½ yards self-made or purchased binding

Supplies & Tools

- All-purpose thread to match fabrics
- Basic sewing tools and supplies

Instructions

1. Prepare templates using pattern pieces given. Cut A–D pieces as directed on each piece for one block; repeat for five A and four B blocks. Cut the A and E pieces for border squares as directed.

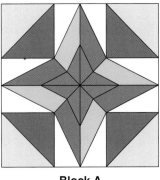

Block A
12" x 12"

Block B
12" x 12"

2. To piece one block, sew a blue floral A to a purple print A; repeat for four A units.

3. Sew D to C to B and DR to CR to BR as shown in Figure 1; repeat for four of each unit. Sew a B-C-D unit to a BR-CR-DR unit as shown in Figure 2; repeat for four units.

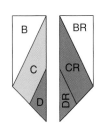

Figure 1
Sew D to C to B and DR
to CR to BR.

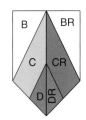

Figure 2
Sew a B-C-D unit to a
BR-CR-DR unit.

4. Join the A units with the B-C-D units as shown in Figure 3 to complete one block; repeat for five A and four B blocks.

Shangri-La Quilt

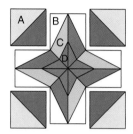

Figure 3
Join the A units with the
B-C-D units as shown to
complete 1 block

5. Arrange the blocks in three rows of three blocks each referring to the Placement Diagram for positioning of blocks. Join the blocks in rows; join rows to complete the pieced center. Press seams in one direction.

6. Cut two strips each 1½" x 36½" and 1½" x 38½" light rose print. Sew the shorter strips to opposite sides and longer strips to the top and bottom of the pieced center; press seams toward strips.

7. Sew a green print E to a rose print E and sew to a purple print A as shown in Figure 4 to make a corner unit; repeat for four corner units.

Figure 4
Sew a green print E to a rose
print E; sew to a purple print A as
shown to make a corner unit.

8. Cut four strips 4½" x 38½" multicolored print. Sew a strip to opposite sides of the pieced center; press seams toward strips.

9. Sew a corner unit to each end of the remaining two strips as shown in Figure 5. Sew these strips to the remaining sides of the pieced center to complete the pieced top.

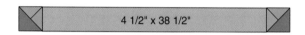

4 1/2" x 38 1/2"

Figure 5
Sew a corner unit to each end
of a 4 1/2" x 38 1/2" strip.

10. Sandwich batting between completed top and prepared backing piece; pin or baste to hold layers together.

11. Quilt as desired by hand or machine.

12. When quilting is complete, trim edges even and remove pins or basting. Bind edges with self-made or purchased binding to finish. ❖

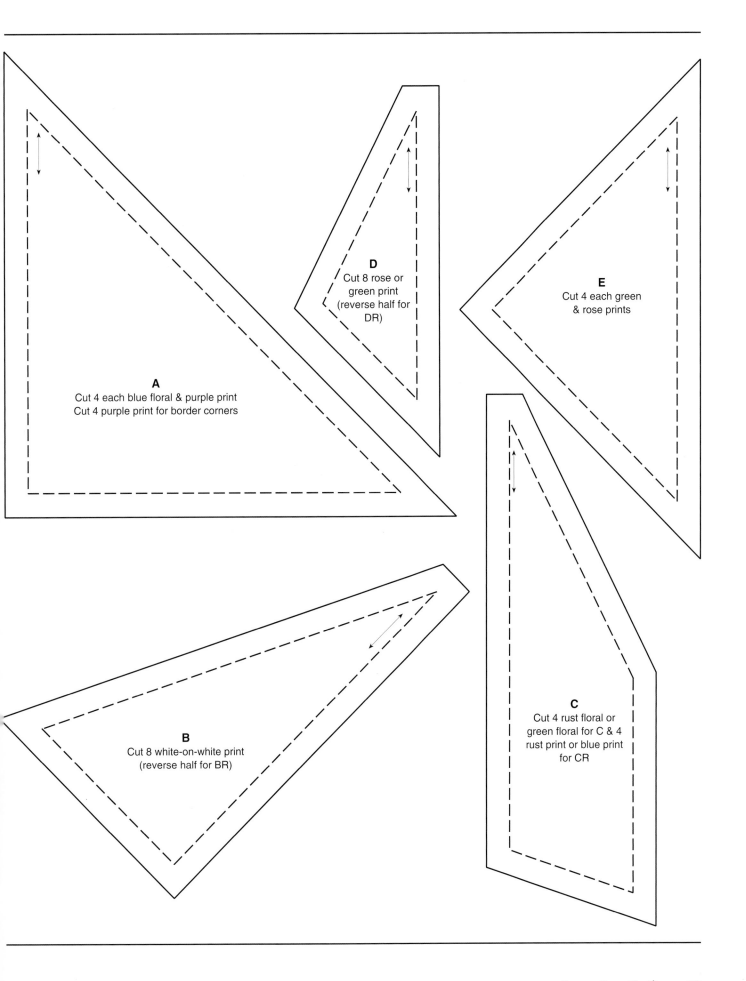

D
Cut 8 rose or
green print
(reverse half for
DR)

E
Cut 4 each green
& rose prints

A
Cut 4 each blue floral & purple print
Cut 4 purple print for border corners

C
Cut 4 rust floral or
green floral for C & 4
rust print or blue print
for CR

B
Cut 8 white-on-white print
(reverse half for BR)

Amish Wedding Ring

BY LINDA DENNER

The traditional Amish Wedding Ring is one of the best known of all quilt patterns, but it is probably one of the most intimidating. With accurate cutting and care in maintaining a perfect ¼" seam allowance, however, the problems should be eliminated. In this scrap version, each of the wedges is a different solid color. Traditionally, the pattern calls for a Four-Patch at the junction of intersecting wedges; in this quilt, there is a small Star block. When you have finished this little sample, you may gather courage to make a queen-size version the next time around.

Amish Wedding Ring

Amish Wedding Ring
Placement Diagram
Approximately 41 1/4" x 41 1/4"

Amish Wedding Ring

Project Specifications

Quilt Size: Approximately 41¼" x 41¼"

Fabric & Batting

- 1½ yards black solid
- Assorted scraps of varied solids
- 1½ yards backing fabric
- Batting 45" x 45"
- 5½ yards self-made or purchased binding

Supplies & Tools

- Matching color all-purpose thread
- 1 spool quilting thread
- Basic sewing supplies and tools and template plastic

Instructions

1. Trace patterns on template plastic. Cut as directed on each piece.

2. Referring to Figure 1, piece 16 star blocks.

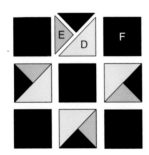

Figure 1
Piece miniature star
blocks as shown.

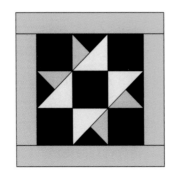

Miniature Star
Placement Diagram
2 5/8" x 2 5/8"

3. Cut 32 strips each 1" x 3⅛" and 1" x 4⅛" using a solid star color. Sew a short strip to opposite sides of each block; press. Sew longer strips to remaining sides; press.

4. Attach two B wedge shapes to each side of a black A piece as shown in Figure 2; repeat for 24 B-A-B units.

Figure 2
Sew B to A to B.

5. Arrange the B-A-B wedge units around the nine center black C sections until you are pleased with the color layout. *Note: I frequently tack a flannel cloth on a wall and press my patchwork on the flannel to temporarily preview the arrangement. Stand back about 5 feet and look at the emerging design. Errors in color placement are more apparent with a vertical display. Reposition the wedges; overlay the miniatures into the arrangement.*

Amish Wedding Ring

6. Working horizontally and from left to right, sew left side B-A-B unit to a C black center. Attach a B-A-B unit to the right side of the C section. Continue in this manner until the three C sections have wedges on their sides, forming the first row, as shown in Figure 3. Repeat for three rows.

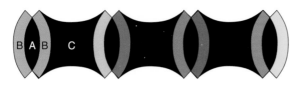

Figure 3
Join pieced units as shown.

7. Sew four star blocks to three B-A-B units to make a row as shown in Figure 4; repeat for four rows.

Figure 4
Sew star blocks and B-A-B units to make rows.

8. Join the star-block rows with the C rows referring to Figure 5. Repeat until all rows are stitched to complete top.

9. Sandwich batting between completed top and prepared backing piece. Pin or baste layers together.

10. Quilt as desired and in the ditch of seams.

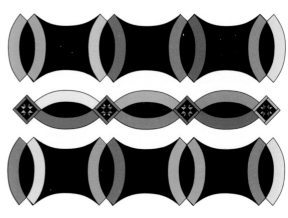

Figure 5
Join the star-block B-A-B rows with the C rows as shown.

11. When quilting is complete, trim edges even. Bind with self-made or purchased binding, mitering corners and overlapping ends. ❖

C
Cut 9 black

Place line on fold

Place line on fold

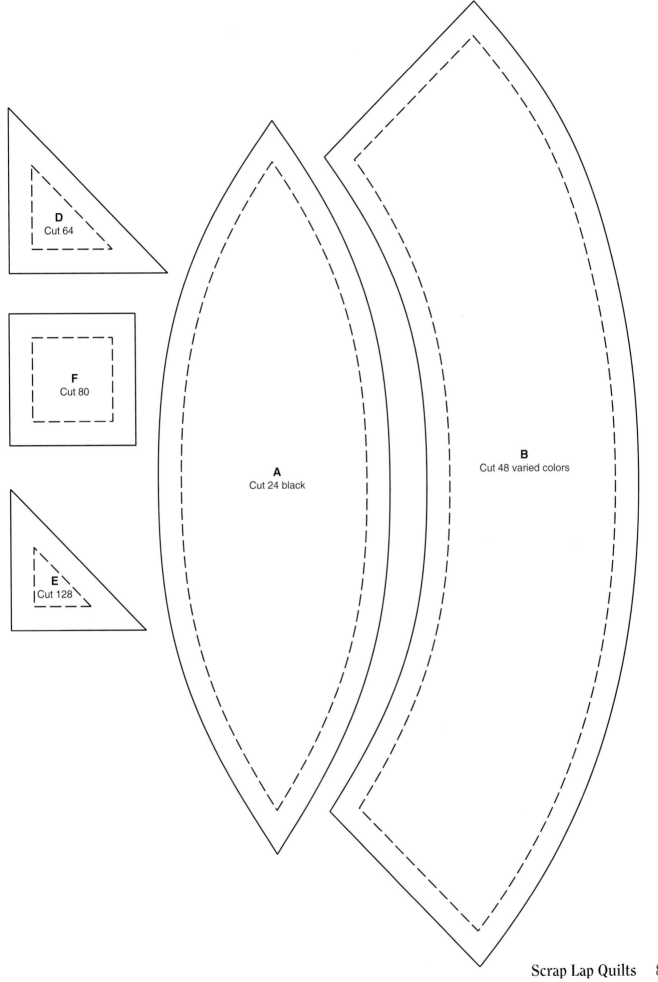

D
Cut 64

F
Cut 80

E
Cut 128

A
Cut 24 black

B
Cut 48 varied colors

Don't Put All Your Eggs in One Basket

BY SUSAN REDSTREAKE GEARY

The designer of this quilt spent over two years collecting prints suitable for baskets. When she had enough prints, she sat down and designed this quilt. All of the baskets are different fat quarters, and other scraps of fabric are used for the chicken body and the nest. Just looking at the quilt, you know how much fun she had making something wonderful out of scraps.

Don't Put All Your Eggs in One Basket

Don't Put All Your Eggs in One Basket
Placement Diagram
42" x 42"

Don't Put All Your Eggs in One Basket

Project Specifications

Quilt Size: 42" x 42"

Block Size: 6" x 6"

Number of Blocks: 23

Fabric & Batting

- 23 different fat quarters of basket fabrics (plaids, wovens, check, etc.)
- 6 (¼-yard) pieces background fabrics (muslin may be used)
- ⅝ yard red print
- ⅓ yard chicken body fabric
- ⅓ yard gold print
- ¼ yard chicken wing and tail fabric
- ⅛ yard nest fabric
- Scraps red and gold for beak, comb and wattle
- Backing 46" x 46"
- Batting 46" x 46"
- 5 yards self-made or purchased binding

Supplies & Tools

- Coordinating all-purpose thread
- Gold embroidery floss for eye
- Basic sewing tools and supplies, rotary cutter, mat and ruler

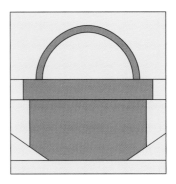

Basket
6" x 6" Block

Instructions

1. Prepare templates for pieced Basket block using pattern pieces given. Cut as directed on each piece for one block; repeat for 23 blocks.

2. To piece one block, sew E and ER to B and add F and FR as shown in Figure 1. Sew G to the F side of the pieced unit. Sew D to each short end of C; sew to the top of the pieced unit as shown in Figure 2.

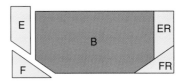

Figure 1
Sew E and ER to B and add F and FR.

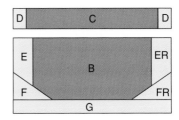

Figure 2
Sew D-C-D to top of pieced unit.

Don't Put All Your Eggs in One Basket

3. Make a template for the Handle Guide. Place guide on A; trace shape as shown in Figure 3. Cut basket handle piece, adding a ¼" seam allowance all around when cutting. Turn edges under; place on A using marked line as a guide for placement. Hand-appliqué handle in place.

Figure 3
Place Handle Guide on A;
mark curved edge.

4. Sew the appliquéd A piece to the previously pieced unit to complete one block as shown in Figure 4; press. Repeat for 23 blocks.

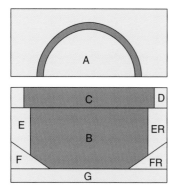

Figure 4
Sew the appliquéd A piece to the
pieced unit to complete 1 block.

5. Cut two 6½" x 6½" background blocks.

6. Arrange the blocks in four rows of five blocks each; join blocks in rows. Join rows; press. Join three blocks with the two 6½" x 6½" background squares to make a row as shown in Figure 5; press. Sew this row to the bottom of the previously pieced section; press.

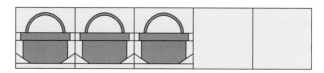

Figure 5
Join 3 blocks with 2 background squares to make bottom row.

7. Prepare templates for chicken pieces, adding a ¼" seam allowance on body piece when cutting.

8. Place tail pieces right sides together; sew all around, leaving a 2" opening to turn. Clip curves; turn right side out. Hand-stitch opening closed. Repeat for wing and comb pieces.

9. Fold beak piece right sides together; sew along one side as shown in Figure 6. Trim point; turn right side out.

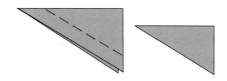

Figure 6
Fold beak; sew along 1 side and turn.

10. Turn under seam allowance on wattle piece; baste or press to hold.

11. Pin chicken body to background blocks referring to the Placement Diagram and photo of project for positioning. Arrange comb, wattle and beak pieces, tucking ends under chicken as marked on chicken pattern; pin in place. Hand-appliqué chicken body to background, turning under seam allowance as you stitch. Catch comb, wattle and beak pieces in appliqué, leaving outside edges of these pieces free. Hand-appliqué wattle and beak pieces in place.

12. For a three-dimensional look, appliqué tail section along tail's left edge, leaving right side loose. Appliqué wing along left side and part way along top.

13. Satin-stitch chicken eye using 4 strands gold embroidery floss referring to the Chicken Body pattern for placement.

14. Cut nest box rectangle from one basket print 2¾" x 12½". Turn under ¼" all around. Appliqué over chicken body along dotted line marked on pattern; press.

15. Cut two strips gold print 2½" x 30½"; sew a strip to the top and bottom of pieced section. Press seams toward strips.

16. Cut two more strips gold print 2½" x 34½"; sew to remaining sides. Press seams toward strips.

17. Cut two strips red print 4½" x 34½"; sew a strip to the top and bottom of pieced center. Press seam toward strips.

18. Cut two more strips red print 4½" x 42½"; sew to remaining sides. Press seams toward strips.

19. Sandwich batting between completed top and prepared backing piece. Pin or baste layers together to hold flat for quilting.

20. Quilt as desired by hand or machine. When quilting is complete, trim edges even. Bind edges with self-made or purchased binding to finish.

21. A sleeve may be added to the top backside for hanging, if desired. ❖

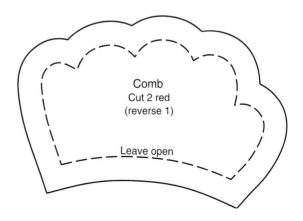

Comb
Cut 2 red
(reverse 1)

Leave open

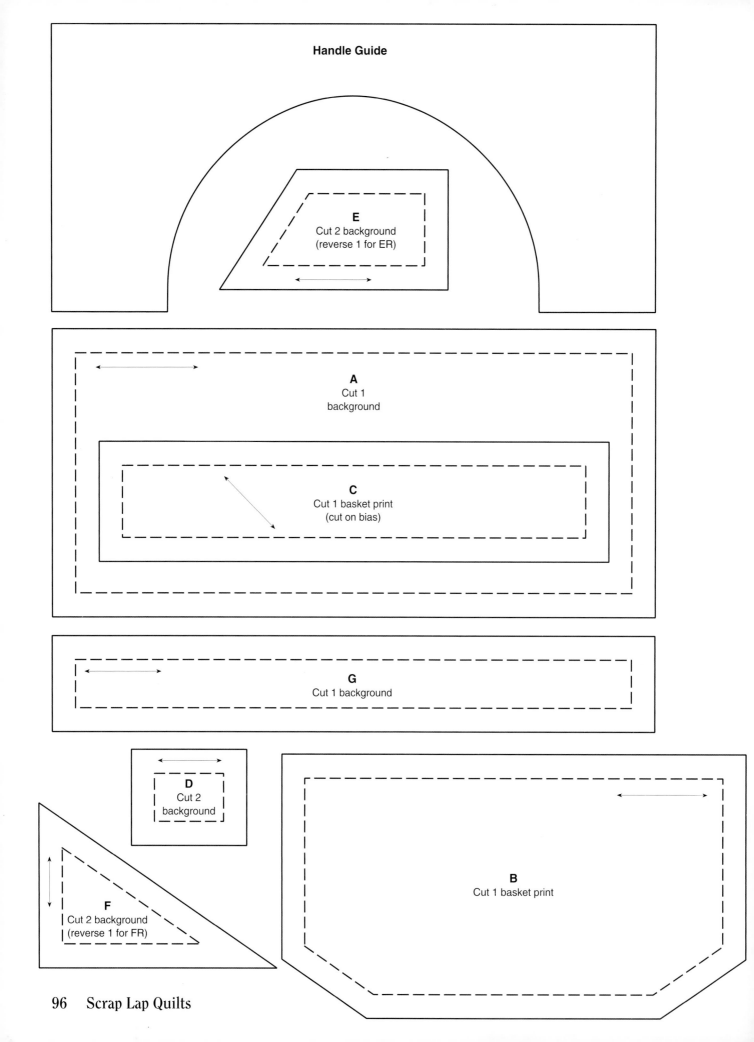

Handle Guide

E
Cut 2 background
(reverse 1 for ER)

A
Cut 1
background

C
Cut 1 basket print
(cut on bias)

G
Cut 1 background

D
Cut 2
background

F
Cut 2 background
(reverse 1 for FR)

B
Cut 1 basket print

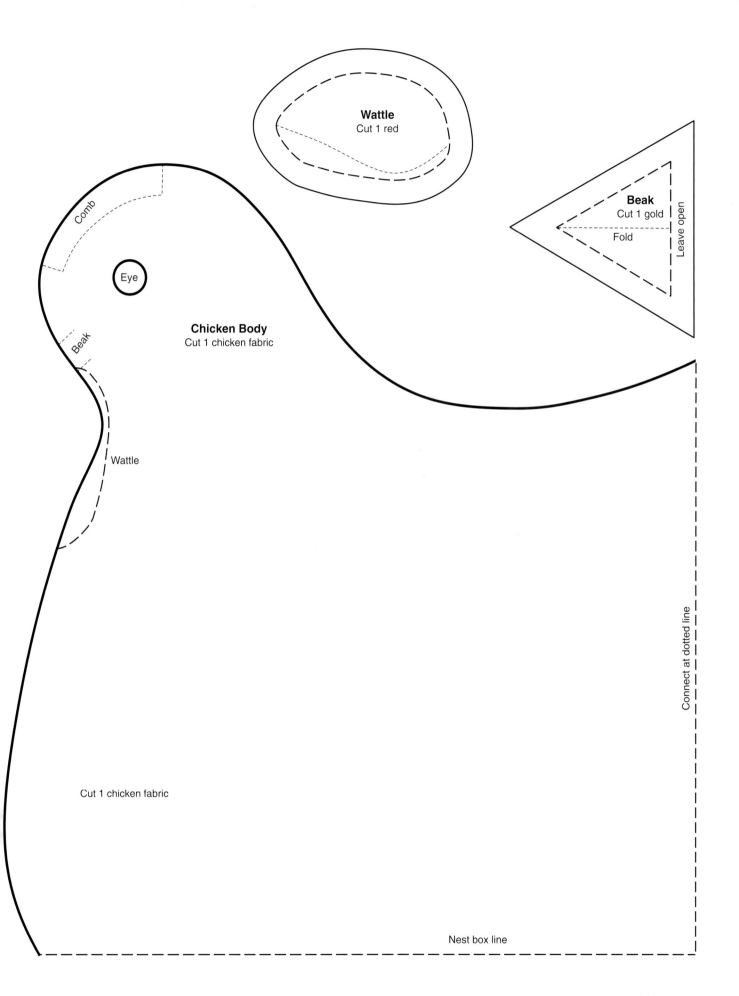

Wattle
Cut 1 red

Beak
Cut 1 gold
Fold
Leave open

Comb

Eye

Beak

Chicken Body
Cut 1 chicken fabric

Wattle

Connect at dotted line

Cut 1 chicken fabric

Nest box line

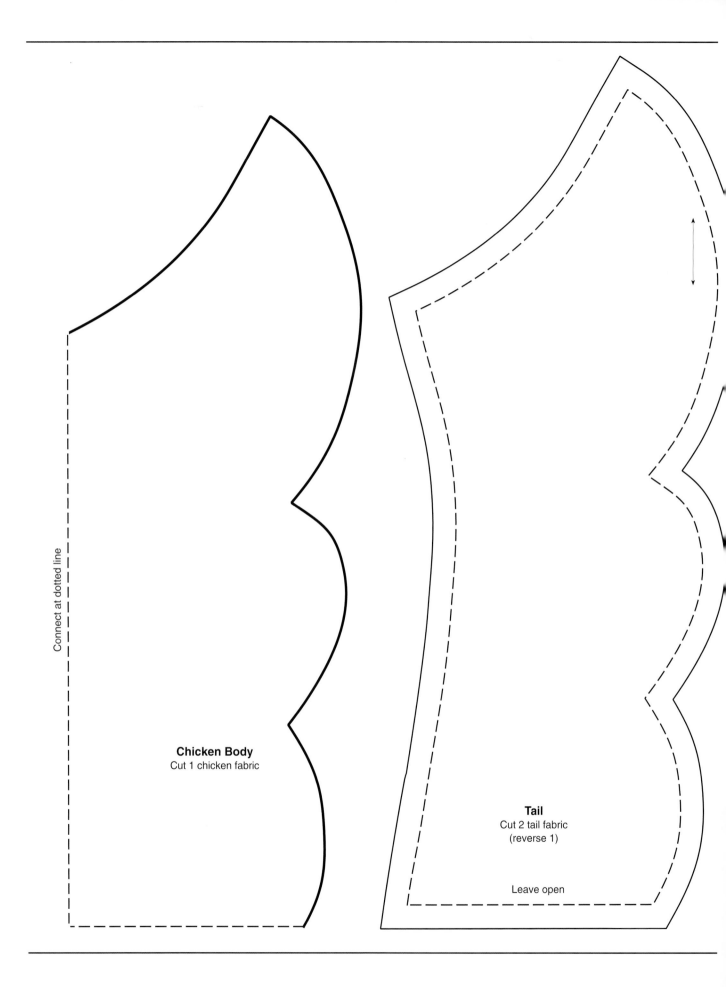

Connect at dotted line

Chicken Body
Cut 1 chicken fabric

Tail
Cut 2 tail fabric
(reverse 1)

Leave open

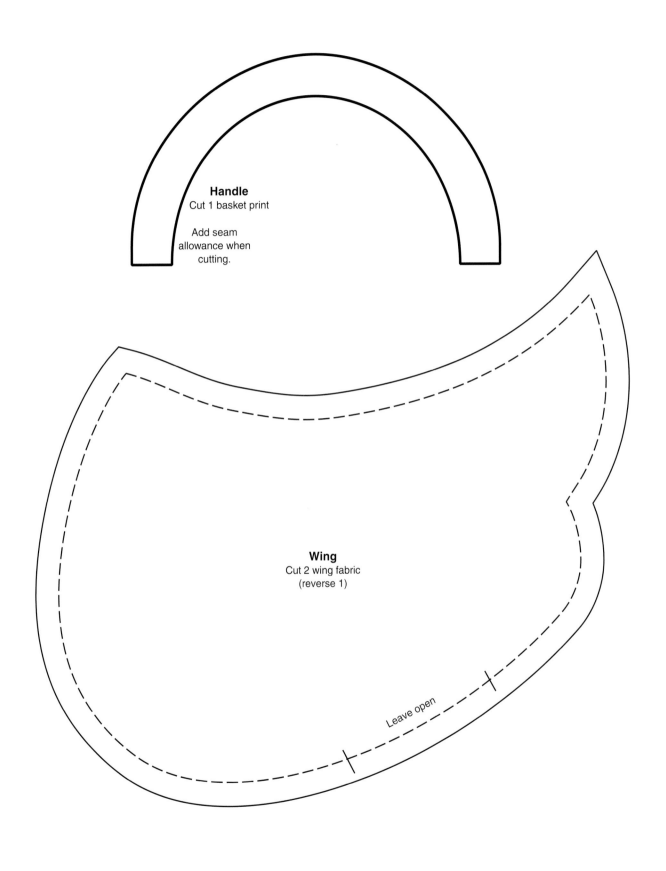

Handle
Cut 1 basket print

Add seam
allowance when
cutting.

Wing
Cut 2 wing fabric
(reverse 1)

Leave open

Butterflies & Blossoms

BY HOLLY DANIELS

The butterflies in this quilt are in the fabric used in the border of the quilt; the blossoms are the ingenious quilt blocks. Similar to a Dresden Plate, the center stars contrast with the gentle curving of the petals. The blossoms are pieced and then appliquéd onto the background blocks in a project that allows you to combine your piecing and appliqué skills to create a lovely lap quilt.

Butterflies & Blossoms

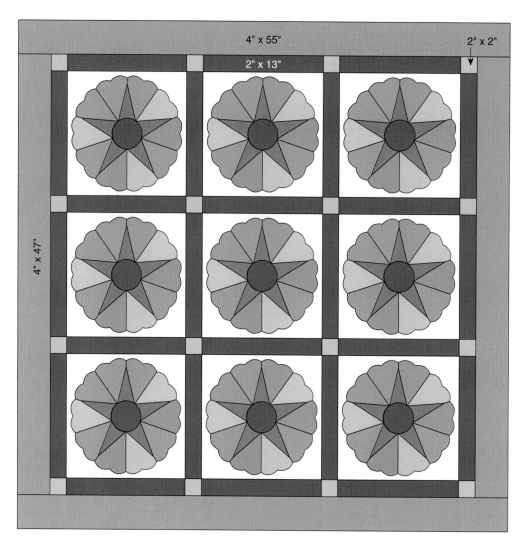

Butterflies & Blossoms
Placement Diagram
55" x 55"

Butterflies & Blossoms

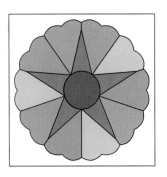

Butterflies & Blossoms
13" x 13" Block

Project Specifications

Quilt Size: 55" x 55"

Block Size: 13" x 13"

Number of Blocks: 9

Fabric & Batting

- 1 strip pink print 2½" by fabric width
- ½ yard blue mottled or solid
- 1 yard blue print
- 1¾ yards butterfly print
- 1½ yards total pink print scraps
- 1¼ yards white solid
- Backing 59" x 59"
- Batting 59" x 59"
- 7 yards self-made or purchased binding

Supplies & Tools

- White and neutral color all-purpose thread
- White quilting thread
- Basic sewing supplies and tools

Instructions

1. Prepare templates using pattern pieces given. Cut as directed on each piece for one block; repeat for nine blocks.

2. Sew A and AR to B as shown in Figure 1; repeat for five units. Press seams toward A pieces. Join

five units to make a ring as shown in Figure 2. Repeat for nine units.

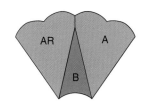

Figure 1
Sew A and AR to
B as shown.

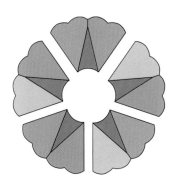

Figure 2
Join A-B units to complete a ring.

3. Cut nine white squares 13½" x 13½". Fold and crease to mark centers.

4. Center a pieced unit on a background square as shown in Figure 3. Hand-appliqué in place, turning edges under as you stitch; repeat for nine blocks.

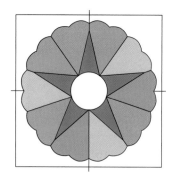

Figure 3
Center pieced units on
13 1/2" x 13 1/2" background block.

5. Turn under edges of the C circle piece. Place over center of an appliquéd block; hand-appliqué in place. Repeat for nine blocks.

6. Carefully trim excess background from underneath appliquéd section to reduce bulk.

7. Cut eight strips blue print 2½" by fabric width. Cut strips into 13½" segments; you will need 24 segments for sashing strips.

8. Cut one 2½" by fabric width pink print strip; cut in 2½" segments. You will need 16 segments for sashing squares.

9. Join three blocks with four 2½" x 13½" sashing strips to make a block row as shown in Figure 4; press seams toward strips. Repeat for three block rows.

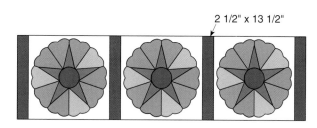

2 1/2" x 13 1/2"

Figure 4
Join 3 blocks with 4 sashing strips to make a block row.

10. Join four 2½" x 2½" pink print squares with three 2½" x 13½" sashing strips to make a sashing row as shown in Figure 5; press seams toward strips. Repeat for four sashing rows.

2 1/2" x 2 1/2"

2 1/2" x 13 1/2"

Figure 5
Join 4 squares with 3 sashing strips to make a sashing row as shown.

11. Join the three block rows with the four sashing rows to complete quilt center referring to Placement Diagram; press seams toward sashing rows.

12. Cut two strips butterfly print 4½" x 47½"; sew to opposite sides of pieced center. Press seams toward strips. Cut two more strips butterfly print 4½" x 55½"; sew to remaining sides of pieced center. Press seams toward strips.

13. Sandwich batting between completed top and prepared backing piece. Pin or baste layers together to hold flat. Quilt as desired by hand or machine using white quilting thread.

14. When quilting is complete, trim edges even. Bind with self-made or purchased binding to finish. ❖

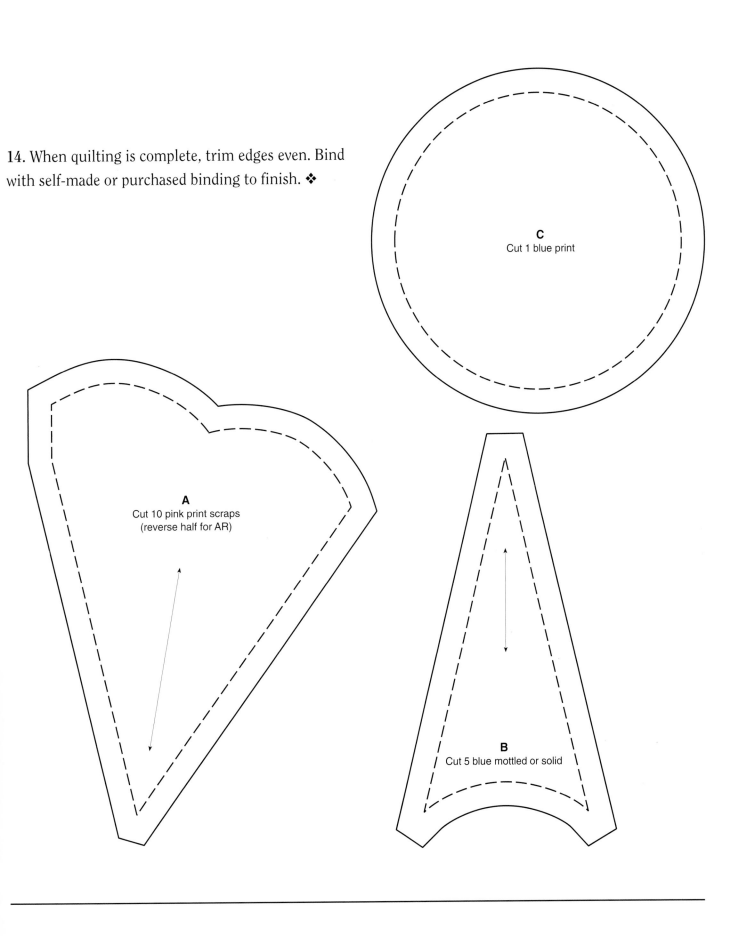

C
Cut 1 blue print

A
Cut 10 pink print scraps
(reverse half for AR)

B
Cut 5 blue mottled or solid

Amish Mosaic

BY LUCY FAZELY

An Amish quilt by definition is one that is made with simple shapes, bright solids and lots of fine quilting. This little quilt fits all of those criteria. There are nine different scraps of bright solids making up half of the 100 squares and enough black fabric to make up the other half of the 100 squares as well as two borders. In addition, the photographed quilt is quilted in the ditch of all seams and a quilting design appears along one of the borders.

Amish Mosaic

Amish Mosaic
Placement Diagram
33 3/4" x 33 3/4"

Amish Mosaic

Project Specifications

Quilt Size: 33¾" x 33¾"

Unit Size: 2⅛" x 2⅛"

Number of Units: 100

Fabric & Batting

- ⅛ yard each pale yellow, bright yellow, peach, light gray, medium purple, dark purple, navy blue and light blue solids
- ½ yard medium blue solid
- 1⅛ yards black solid
- Backing 38" x 38"
- Batting 38" x 38"
- 4 yards self-made or purchased binding

Supplies & Tools

- All-purpose thread to match fabrics
- Basic sewing tools and supplies, water-erasable marker or pencil, rotary cutter, mat and ruler

Instructions

1. Cut the following 3" x 3" squares: 50 black, two pale yellow, four bright yellow, six peach, eight light gray, 10 light blue, eight medium blue, six medium purple, four dark purple and two navy blue.

2. Cut each square in half on one diagonal to make triangles as shown in Figure 1.

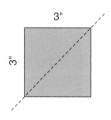

Figure 1
Cut each square in half
on 1 diagonal.

3. With right sides together, pair each black triangle with a colored triangle. Sew together along longest edge as shown in Figure 2. Press each triangle set flat and then press seam allowances toward black fabric. Trim excess seam allowance at each corner to reduce bulk.

Figure 2
Sew a black triangle to a
colored triangle; trim
excess at corners.

4. Lay out pieced units in rows referring to Figure 3 for color positioning. Join units in rows; join rows to complete pieced center. Press seams in one direction.

5. Cut eight strips black solid 2" x 37" and four strips medium blue solid 3½" x 37". Sew a black solid strip to each side of a medium blue strip; press seams toward black solid. Repeat for four strip sets. Sew

Amish Mosaic

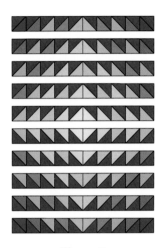

Figure 3
Arrange pieced units
in rows as shown.

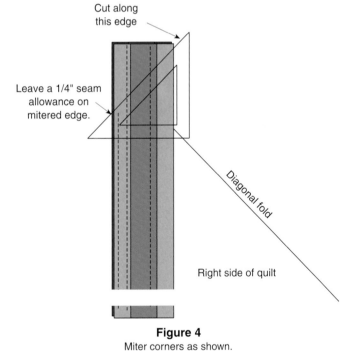

Figure 4
Miter corners as shown.

strip sets to sides of pieced center, mitering corners as shown in Figure 4; press seams toward strips.

6. Mark medium blue border with quilting design given using a water-erasable marker or pencil. *Note: Quilt shown was also machine-quilted in the ditch of all seams.*

7. Sandwich batting between completed top and prepared backing piece; pin or baste layers together to hold flat.

8. Quilt on marked lines or as desired by hand or machine. When quilting is complete, trim edges even; remove pins or basting.

9. Bind edges with self-made or purchased binding to finish. ❖

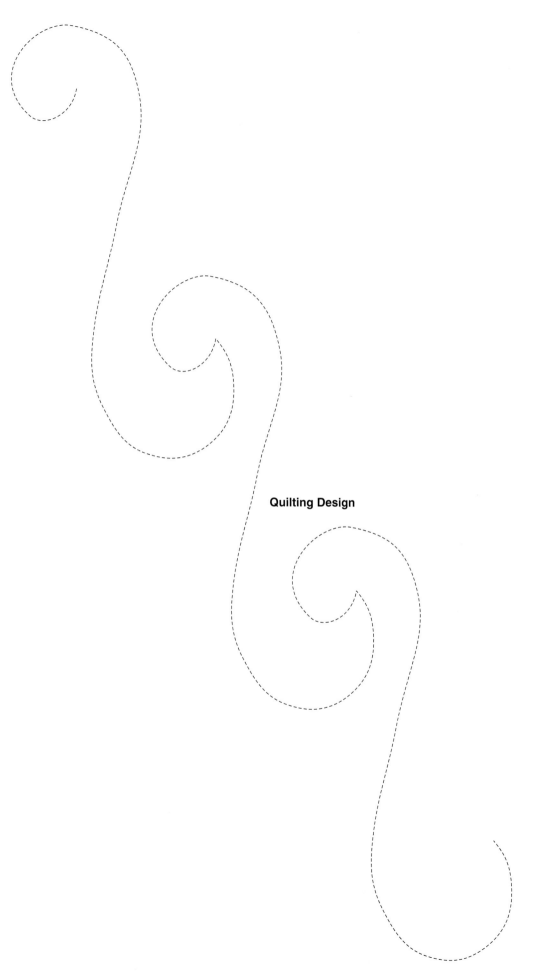

Quilting Design

Windmill Scrappy Fun

BY LINDA DENNER

This project is perfect for a beginner because of its simple construction, or for quilters who have been sewing for a long time and have lots of scraps to use. The quilt designer used navy as a background color because she felt that it offered a great opportunity for high contrast. The blades were made with prints ranging from hot to cool colors, working from red through purple and aqua. Once the blades are cut out, the quilt top could be put together in a delightful afternoon.

Project Specifications

Quilt Size: 42" x 53¼"
Block Size: 8" x 8"
Number of Blocks: 18

Fabric & Batting

- Fat eighths of 18 prints or 6" squares of 36 prints
- ¼ yard bright-colored print
- 2 yards total assorted navy prints
- Backing 46" x 57"
- Batting 46" x 57"
- 5¾ yards self-made or purchased binding

Supplies & Tools

- All-purpose thread to match fabrics

Windmill
8" x 8" Block

- Basic sewing tools and supplies, pencil, rotary cutter, mat and ruler

Instructions

1. Prepare template for A using pattern piece given; cut as directed on the piece. Be careful not to

Windmill Scrappy Fun

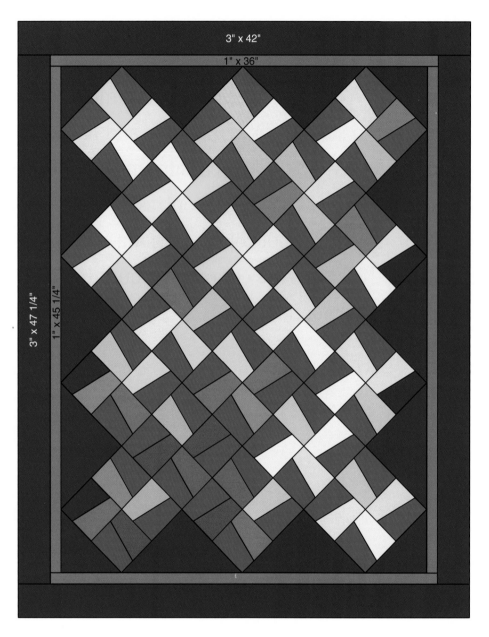

Windmill Scrappy Fun
Placement Diagram
42" x 53 1/4"

reverse the template. If cutting through several layers of fabric, be sure fabrics are all stacked in the same direction.

2. To piece one block, join two A pieces as shown in Figure 1 to complete an A unit; repeat for four A units. Join the units to complete one block as shown in Figure 2; repeat for 18 blocks. *Note: Some of the blocks are made using dark and medium A pieces for the units while others use dark and light A pieces. Refer to the photo of the project and the Placement Diagram for positioning of blocks and colors.*

Figure 1
Join 2 A pieces
as shown to
complete an
A unit.

Figure 2
Join 4 A units to
complete 1 block.

3. Cut three squares navy prints 12⅝" x 12⅝" for B; cut each square on both diagonals to make 12 B triangles. Discard two B triangles.

4. Cut two squares navy prints 6⅝" x 6⅝" for C. Cut each square on one diagonal to make four C triangles.

Figure 3
Arrange the blocks
in diagonal rows as shown;
add B and C triangles.

5. Arrange the blocks in diagonal rows as shown in Figure 3. Join the blocks in rows. Sew B triangles to the end of rows; join the rows. Sew C triangles to each corner; press seams in one direction.

6. Cut two strips each 1½" x 36½" and 1½" x 45¾" bright-colored print. Sew the longer strips to opposite sides and shorter strips to the top and bottom of the pieced top; press seams toward strips.

7. Piece two strips each 3½" x 42½" and 3½" x 47¾" navy prints. Sew the longer strips to opposite sides

Windmill Scrappy Fun

and shorter strips to the top and bottom of the pieced top; press seams toward strips.

8. Sandwich batting between the prepared backing and completed top; pin or baste to hold.

9. Quilt as desired by hand or machine. *Note: The sample was machine-quilted in a meandering pattern in A pieces using all-purpose thread to match A fabrics. The borders were machine-quilted using navy thread in a leaf pattern.*

10. Trim backing and batting even with top; remove pins or basting.

11. Bind edges using self-made or purchased binding to finish. ❖

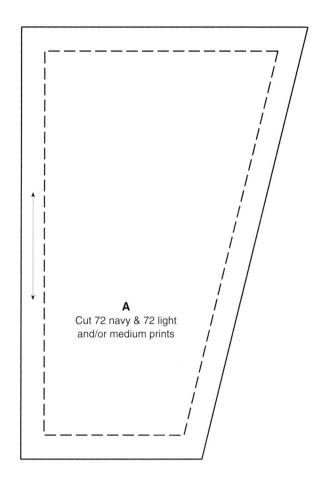

A
Cut 72 navy & 72 light
and/or medium prints

General Instructions

Quiltmaking Basics

Materials & Supplies

Fabrics

Fabric Choices. Quilts and quilted projects combine fabrics of many types. Use same-fiber-content fabrics when making quilted items, if possible.

Buying Fabrics. One hundred percent cotton fabrics are recommended for making quilts. Choose colors similar to those used in the quilts shown or colors of your own preference. Most quilt designs depend more on contrast of values than on the colors used to create the design.

Preparing the Fabric for Use. Fabrics may be prewashed depending on your preference. Whether you prewash or not, be sure your fabrics are colorfast and won't run onto each other when washed after use.

Fabric Grain. Fabrics are woven with threads going in a crosswise and lengthwise direction. The threads cross at right angles—the more threads per inch, the stronger the fabric.

The crosswise threads will stretch a little. The lengthwise threads will not stretch at all. Cutting the fabric at a 45-degree angle to the crosswise and lengthwise threads produces a bias edge which stretches a great deal when pulled (Figure 1).

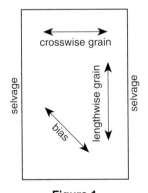

Figure 1
Drawing shows lengthwise, crosswise and bias threads.

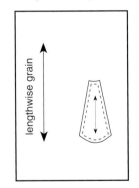

Figure 2
Place the template with marked arrow on the lengthwise grain of the fabric.

If templates are given with patterns in this book, pay careful attention to the grain lines marked with arrows. These arrows indicate that the piece should be placed on the lengthwise grain with the arrow running on one thread. Although it is not necessary to examine the fabric and find a thread to match to, it is important to try to place the arrow with the lengthwise grain of the fabric (Figure 2).

Thread

For most piecing, good-quality cotton or cotton-covered polyester is the thread of choice. Inexpensive polyester threads are not recommended because they can cut the fibers of cotton fabrics.

Choose a color thread that will match or blend with the fabrics in your quilt. For projects pieced with dark and light color fabrics choose a neutral thread color, such as a medium gray, as a compromise between colors. Test by pulling a sample seam.

Batting

Batting is the material used to give a quilt loft or thickness. It also adds warmth.

Batting size is listed in inches for each pattern to reflect the size needed to complete the quilt according to the instructions. Purchase the size large enough to cut the size you need for the quilt of your choice.

Some qualities to look for in batting are drapability, resistance to fiber migration, loft and softness.

Tools & Equipment

There are few truly essential tools and little equipment required for quiltmaking. Basics include needles (hand-sewing and quilting betweens), pins (long, thin, sharp pins are best), sharp scissors or shears, a thimble, template materials (plastic or cardboard), marking tools (chalk marker, water-erasable pen and a No. 2 pencil are a few) and a quilting frame or hoop. For piecing and/or quilting by machine, add a sewing machine to the list.

Other sewing basics such as a seam ripper, pincushion, measuring tape and an iron are also necessary. For choosing colors

General Instructions

or quilting designs for your quilt, or for designing your own quilt, it is helpful to have on hand graph paper, tracing paper, colored pencils or markers and a ruler.

For making strip-pieced quilts, a rotary cutter, mat and specialty rulers are often used. We recommend an ergonomic rotary cutter, a large self-healing mat and several rulers. If you can choose only one size, a 6" x 24" marked in ⅛" or ¼" increments is recommended.

Construction Methods

Traditional Templates. While some quilt instructions in this book use rotary-cut strips and quick sewing methods, many patterns require a template. Templates are like the pattern pieces used to sew a garment. They are used to cut the fabric pieces that make up the quilt top. There are two types—templates that include a ¼" seam allowance and those that don't.

Choose the template material and the pattern. Transfer the pattern shapes to the template material with a sharp No. 2 lead pencil. Write the pattern name, piece letter or number, grain line and number to cut for one block or whole quilt on each piece as shown in Figure 3.

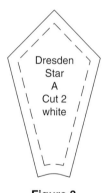

Figure 3
Mark each template with the pattern name and piece identification.

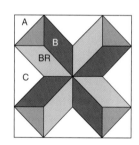

Figure 4
This pattern uses reversed pieces.

Some patterns require a reversed piece (Figure 4). These patterns are labeled with an R after the piece letter; for example, B and BR. To reverse a template, first cut it with the labeled side up and then with the labeled side down. Compare these to the right and left fronts of a blouse. When making a garment, you accomplish reversed pieces when cutting the pattern on two

layers of fabric placed with right sides together. This can be done when cutting templates as well.

If cutting one layer of fabric at a time, first trace the template onto the backside of the fabric with the marked side down; turn the template over with the marked side up to make reverse pieces.

Hand-Piecing Basics. When hand-piecing it is easier to begin with templates that do not include the ¼" seam allowance. Place the template on the wrong side of the fabric, lining up the marked grain line with lengthwise or crosswise fabric grain. If the piece does not have to be reversed, place with labeled side up. Trace around shape; move, leaving ½" between the shapes, and mark again.

When you have marked the appropriate number of pieces, cut out pieces, leaving ¼" beyond marked line all around each piece.

To join two units, place the patches with right sides together. Stick a pin in at the beginning of the seam through both fabric patches, matching the beginning points (Figure 5); for hand-piecing, the seam begins on the traced line, not at the edge of the fabric (see Figure 6).

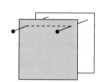

Figure 5
Stick a pin through fabrics to match the beginning of the seam.

Figure 6
Begin hand-piecing at seam, not at the edge of the fabric. Continue stitching along seam line.

Thread a sharp needle; knot one strand of the thread at the end. Remove the pin and insert the needle in the hole; make a short stitch and then a backstitch right over the first stitch. Continue making short stitches with several stitches on the needle at one time. As you stitch, check the back piece often to assure accurate stitching on the seam line. Take a stitch at the end of the seam; backstitch and knot at the same time as shown in Figure 7. Seams on hand-pieced fabric patches may be finger-pressed toward the darker fabric.

To sew units together, pin fabric patches together, matching seams. Sew as above except where seams meet; at these

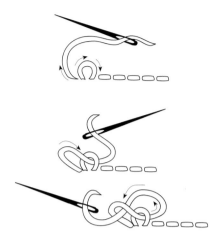

Figure 7
Make a loop in backstitch to make a knot.

intersections, backstitch, go through seam to next piece and backstitch again to secure seam joint.

Not all pieced blocks can be stitched with straight seams or in rows. Some patterns require set-in pieces. To begin a set-in seam, pin one side of the square to the proper side of the star point with right sides together, matching corners. Start stitching at the seam line on the outside point; stitch on the marked seam line to the end of the seam line at the center referring to Figure 8.

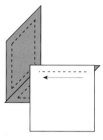

Figure 8
To set a square into a diamond point, match seams and stitch from outside edge to center.

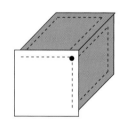

Figure 9
Continue stitching the adjacent side of the square to the next diamond shape in 1 seam from center to outside as shown.

Bring around the adjacent side and pin to the next star point, matching seams. Continue the stitching line from the adjacent seam through corners and to the outside edge of the square as shown in Figure 9.

Machine-Piecing. If making templates, include the ¼" seam allowance on the template for machine-piecing. Place template

on the wrong side of the fabric as for hand-piecing except butt pieces against one another when tracing.

Set machine on 2.5 or 12–15 stitches per inch. Join pieces as for hand-piecing for set-in seams; but for other straight seams, begin and end sewing at the end of the fabric patch sewn as shown in Figure

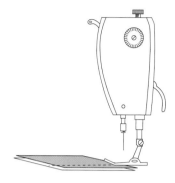

Figure 10
Begin machine-piecing at the end of the piece, not at the end of the seam.

10. No backstitching is necessary when machine-stitching.

Join units as for hand-piecing referring to the piecing diagrams where needed.

Chain piecing (Figure 11—sewing several like units before sewing other units) saves time by eliminating beginning and ending stitches.

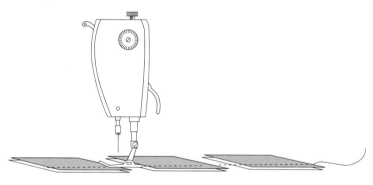

Figure 11
Units may be chain-pieced to save time.

When joining machine-pieced units, match seams against each other with seam allowances pressed in opposite directions to reduce bulk and make perfect matching of seams possible (Figure 12).

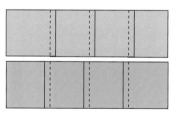

Figure 12
Sew machine-pieced units with seams pressed in opposite directions.

Quick-Cutting. Templates can be completely eliminated when using a rotary cutter with a plastic ruler and mat to cut fabric strips.

General Instructions

When rotary-cutting strips, straighten raw edges of fabric by folding fabric in fourths across the width as shown in Figure 13. Press down flat; place ruler on fabric square with edge of fabric and make one cut from the folded edge to the outside edge. If strips are not straightened, a wavy strip will result as shown in Figure 14.

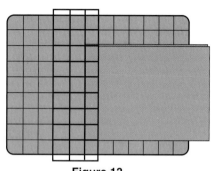

Figure 13
Fold fabric and straighten as shown.

Figure 14
Wavy strips result if fabric is not straightened before cutting.

Always cut away from your body, holding the ruler firmly with the non-cutting hand. Keep fingers away from the edge of the ruler as it is easy for the rotary cutter to slip and jump over the edge of the ruler if cutting is not properly done.

If a square is required for the pattern, it can be subcut from a strip as shown in Figure 15.

Figure 15
If cutting squares, cut proper-width strip into same-width segments. Here, a 2" strip is cut into 2" segments to create 2" squares. These squares finish at 1 1/2" when sewn.

If you need right triangles with the straight grain on the short sides, you can use the same method, but you need to figure out how wide to cut the strip. Measure the finished size of one short side of the triangle. Add ⅞" to this size for seam allowance. Cut fabric strips this width; cut the strips into the same increment to create squares. Cut the squares on the diagonal to produce triangles. For example, if you need a triangle with a 2" finished height, cut the strips 2⅞" by the width of the

fabric. Cut the strips into 2⅞" squares. Cut each square on the diagonal to produce the correct-size triangle with the grain on the short sides (Figure 16).

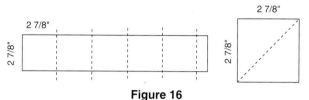

Figure 16
Cut 2" (finished size) triangles from 2 7/8" squares as shown.

Triangles sewn together to make squares are called half-square triangles or triangle/squares. When joined, the triangle/square unit has the straight of grain on all outside edges of the block.

Another method of making triangle/squares is shown in Figure 17. Layer two squares with right sides together; draw a diagonal line through the center. Stitch ¼" on both sides of the line. Cut apart on the drawn line to reveal two stitched triangle/squares.

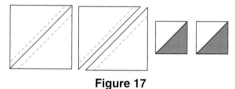

Figure 17
Mark a diagonal line on the square; stitch 1/4" on each side of the line. Cut on line to reveal stitched triangle/squares.

If you need triangles with the straight of grain on the diagonal, such as for fill-in triangles on the outside edges of a diagonal-set quilt, the procedure is a bit different.

To make these triangles, a square is cut on both diagonals; thus, the straight of grain is on the longest or diagonal side (Figure 18). To figure out the size to cut the square, add 1¼" to the needed finished size of the longest side of the triangle. For example, if you need a triangle with a 12" finished diagonal, cut a 13¼" square.

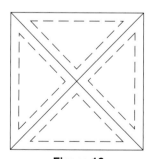

Figure 18
Add 1 1/4" to the finished size of the longest side of the triangle needed and cut on both diagonals to make a quarter-square triangle.

If templates are given, use their measurments to cut fabric strips to correspond with that measurement. The template may be used on the strip to cut pieces quickly. Strip cutting works best for squares, triangles, rectangles and diamonds. Odd-shaped templates are difficult to cut in multiple layers or using a rotary cutter.

Quick-Piecing Method. Lay pieces to be joined under the presser foot of the sewing machine right sides together. Sew an exact ¼" seam allowance to the end of the piece; place another unit right next to the first one and continue sewing, adding a piece after every stitched piece, until all of the pieces are used up (Figure 19).

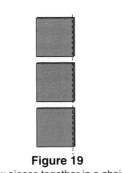

Figure 19
Sew pieces together in a chain.

When sewing is finished, cut threads joining the pieces apart. Press seam toward the darker fabric.

Appliqué

Appliqué. Appliqué is the process of applying one piece of fabric on top of another for decorative or functional purposes.

Making Templates. Most appliqué designs given here are shown as full-size drawings for the completed designs. The drawings show dotted lines to indicate where one piece overlaps another. Other marks indicate placement of embroidery stitches for decorative purposes such as eyes, lips, flowers, etc.

For hand appliqué, trace each template onto the right side of the fabric with template right side up. Cut around shape, adding a ⅛"–¼" seam allowance.

Before the actual appliqué process begins, cut the background block. If you have a full-size drawing of the design, it might help you to draw on the background block to help with placement.

Transfer the design to a large piece of tracing paper. Place the paper on top of the design; use masking tape to hold in place. Trace design onto paper.

If you don't have a light box, tape the pattern on a window; center the background block on top and tape in place. Trace the design onto the background block with a water-erasable marker or light lead or chalk pencil. This drawing will mark exactly where the fabric pieces should be placed on the background block.

Hand Appliqué. Traditional hand appliqué uses a template made from the desired finished shape without seam allowance added.

After fabric is prepared, trace the desired shape onto the right side of the fabric with a water-erasable marker or light lead or chalk pencil. Leave at least ½" between design motifs when tracing to allow for the seam allowance when cutting out the shapes.

When the desired number of shapes needed has been drawn on the fabric pieces, cut out shapes leaving ⅛"–¼" all around drawn line for turning under.

Turn the shape's edges over on the drawn or stitched line. When turning in concave curves, clip to seams and baste the seam allowance over as shown in Figure 20.

Figure 20
Concave curves should be clipped before turning as shown.

During the actual appliqué process, you may be layering one shape on top of another. Where two fabrics overlap, the underneath piece does not have to be turned under or stitched down.

If possible, trim away the underneath fabric when the block is finished by carefully cutting away the background from underneath and then cutting away unnecessary layers to reduce bulk and avoid shadows from darker fabrics showing through on light fabrics.

For hand appliqué, position the fabric shapes on the background block and pin or baste them in place. Using a blind stitch or appliqué stitch, sew pieces in place with matching thread and small stitches. Start with background pieces first and work up to foreground pieces. Appliqué the pieces in place on the background in numerical order, if given, layering as necessary.

Machine Appliqué. There are several products available to help make the machine-appliqué process easier and faster.

Fusible transfer web is a commercial product similar to iron-on interfacings except it has two sticky sides. It is used to

General Instructions

adhere appliqué shapes to the background with heat. Paper is adhered to one side of the web.

To use, reverse pattern and draw shapes onto the paper side of the web; cut, leaving a margin around each shape. Place on the wrong side of the chosen fabric; fuse in place referring to the manufacturer's instructions. Cut out shapes on the drawn line. Peel off the paper and fuse in place on the background fabric. Transfer any detail lines to the fabric shapes. This process adds a little bulk or stiffness to the appliquéd shape and makes hand-quilting through the layers difficult.

For successful machine appliqué a tear-off stabilizer is recommended. This product is placed under the background fabric while machine appliqué is being done. It is torn away when the work is finished. This kind of stabilizer keeps the background fabric from pulling during the machine-appliqué process.

During the actual machine-appliqué process, you will be layering one shape on top of another. Where two fabrics overlap, the underneath piece does not have to be turned under or stitched down.

Thread the top of the machine with thread to match the fabric patches or with threads that coordinate or contrast with fabrics. Rayon thread is a good choice when a sheen is desired on the finished appliqué stitches. Do not use rayon thread in the bobbin; use all-purpose thread.

When all machine work is complete, remove stabilizer from the back referring to the manufacturer's instructions.

Putting It All Together

Finishing the Top
Settings. Most quilts are made by sewing individual blocks together in rows that, when joined, create a design. There are several other methods used to join blocks. Sometimes the setting choice is determined by the block's design. For example, a House block should be placed upright on a quilt, not sideways or upside down.

Plain blocks can be alternated with pieced or appliquéd blocks in a straight set. Making a quilt using plain blocks saves time; half the number of pieced or appliquéd blocks are needed to make the same-size quilt as shown in Figure 1.

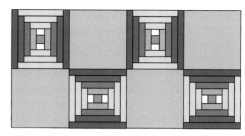

Figure 1
Alternate plain blocks with pieced blocks to save time.

Adding Borders. Borders are an integral part of the quilt and should complement the colors and designs used in the quilt center. Borders frame a quilt just like a mat and frame do a picture.

If fabric strips are added for borders, they may be mitered or butted at the corners as shown in Figures 2 and 3. To determine the size for butted border strips, measure across the center of the completed quilt top from one side raw edge to the other side raw edge. This measurement will include a ¼" seam allowance.

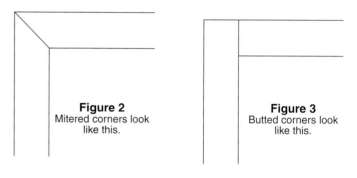

Figure 2
Mitered corners look like this.

Figure 3
Butted corners look like this.

Cut two border strips that length by the chosen width of the border. Sew these strips to the top and bottom of the pieced center referring to Figure 4. Press the seam allowance toward the border strips.

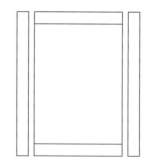

Figure 4
Sew border strips to opposite sides; sew remaining 2 strips to remaining sides to make butted corners.

Measure across the completed quilt top at the center, from top raw edge to bottom raw edge, including the two border strips already added. Cut two border strips that length by the chosen width of the border. Sew a strip to each of the two remaining sides as shown in Figure 4. Press the seams toward the border strips.

To make mitered corners, measure the quilt as before. To this add twice the width of the border and ½" for seam allowances to determine the length of the strips. Repeat for opposite sides. Sew on each strip, stopping stitching ¼" from corner, leaving the remainder of the strip dangling.

Press corners at a 45-degree angle to form a crease. Stitch from the inside quilt corner to the outside on the creased line. Trim excess away after stitching and press mitered seams open (Figures 5–7).

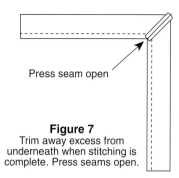

Figure 7
Trim away excess from underneath when stitching is complete. Press seams open.

Carefully press the entire piece, including the pieced center. Avoid pulling and stretching while pressing, which would distort shapes.

Getting Ready to Quilt

Choosing a Quilting Design. If you choose to hand- or machine-quilt your finished top, you will need to select a design for quilting.

There are several types of quilting designs, some of which may not have to be marked. The easiest of the unmarked designs is in-the-ditch quilting. Here the quilting stitches are placed in the valley created by the seams joining two pieces together or next to the edge of an appliqué design. There is no need to mark a top for in-the-ditch quilting. Machine quilters choose this option because the stitches are not as obvious on the finished quilt. (Figure 8).

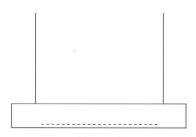

Figure 5
For mitered corner, stitch strip, stopping 1/4" from corner seam.

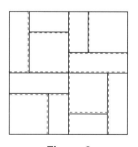

Figure 8
In-the-ditch quilting is done in the seam that joins 2 pieces.

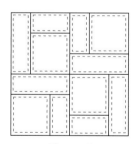

Figure 9
Outline-quilting 1/4" away from seam is a popular choice for quilting.

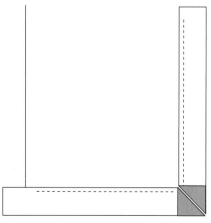

Figure 6
Fold and press corner to make a 45-degree angle.

Outline-quilting ¼" or more away from seams or appliqué shapes is another no-mark alternative (Figure 9) that prevents having to sew through the layers made by seams, thus making stitching easier.

General Instructions

If you are not comfortable eyeballing the ¼" (or other distance), masking tape is available in different widths and is helpful to place on straight-edge designs to mark the quilting line. If using masking tape, place the tape right up against the seam and quilt close to the other edge.

Meander or free-motion quilting by machine fills in open spaces and doesn't require marking. It is fun and easy to stitch as shown in Figure 10.

Figure 10
Machine meander quilting
fills in large spaces.

Marking the Top for Quilting.
If you choose a fancy or allover design for quilting, you will need to transfer the design to your quilt top before layering with the backing and batting. You may use a sharp medium-lead or silver pencil on light background fabrics. Test the pencil marks to guarantee that they will wash out of your quilt top when quilting is complete; or be sure your quilting stitches cover the pencil marks. Mechanical pencils with very fine points may be used successfully to mark quilts.

Manufactured quilt-design templates are available in many designs and sizes and are cut out of a durable plastic template material that is easy to use.

To make a permanent quilt-design template, choose a template material on which to transfer the design. See-through plastic is the best as it will let you place the design while allowing you to see where it is in relation to your quilt design without moving it. Place the design on the quilt top where you want it and trace around it with your marking tool. Pick up the quilting template and place again; repeat marking.

No matter what marking method you use, remember—the marked lines should never show on the finished quilt. When the top is marked, it is ready for layering.

Preparing the Quilt Backing. The quilt backing is a very important feature of your quilt. The materials listed for each quilt in this book includes the size requirements for the backing, not the yardage needed. Exceptions to this are when the backing fabric is also used on the quilt top and yardage is given for that fabric.

A backing is generally cut at least 4" larger than the quilt top or 2" larger on all sides. For a 64" x 78" finished quilt, the backing would need to be at least 68" x 82".

To avoid having the seam across the center of the quilt backing, cut or tear one of the right-length pieces in half and sew half to each side of the second piece as shown in Figure 11.

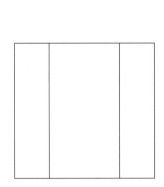

Figure 11
Center 1 backing piece
with a piece on each side.

Figure 12
Horizontal seams may be
used on backing pieces.

Quilts that need a backing more than 88" wide may be pieced in horizontal pieces as shown in Figure 12.

Layering the Quilt Sandwich. Layering the quilt top with the batting and backing is time-consuming. Open the batting several days before you need it and place over a bed or flat on the floor to help flatten the creases caused from its being folded up in the bag for so long.

Iron the backing piece, folding in half both vertically and horizontally and pressing to mark centers.

If you will not be quilting on a frame, place the backing right side down on a clean floor or table. Start in the center and push any wrinkles or bunches flat. Use masking tape to tape the edges to the floor or large clips to hold the backing to the edges of the table. The backing should be taut.

Place the batting on top of the backing, matching centers using fold lines as guides; flatten out any wrinkles. Trim the batting to the same size as the backing.

Fold the quilt top in half lengthwise and place on top of the batting, wrong side against the batting, matching centers. Unfold quilt and, working from the center to the outside edges, smooth out any wrinkles or lumps.

To hold the quilt layers together for quilting, baste by hand or use safety pins. If basting by hand, thread a long thin needle with a long piece of unknotted white or off-white thread. Starting in the center and leaving a long tail, make 4"–6" stitches toward the outside edge of the quilt top, smoothing as you baste. Start at the center again and work toward the outside as shown in Figure 13.

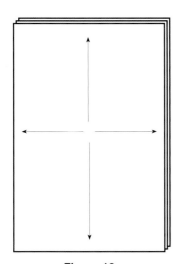

Figure 13
Baste from the center to the outside edges.

If quilting by machine, you may prefer to use safety pins for holding your fabric sandwich together. Start in the center of the quilt and pin to the outside, leaving pins open until all are placed. When you are satisfied that all layers are smooth, close the pins.

Quilting

Hand Quilting. Hand quilting is the process of placing stitches through the quilt top, batting and backing to hold them together. While it is a functional process, it also adds beauty and loft to the finished quilt.

To begin, thread a sharp between needle with an 18" piece of quilting thread. Tie a small knot in the end of the thread. Position the needle about ½" to 1" away from the starting point on quilt top. Sink the needle through the top into the batting layer but not through the backing. Pull the needle up at the starting point

of the quilting design. Pull the needle and thread until the knot sinks through the top into the batting (Figure 14).

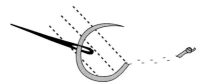

Figure 14
Start the needle through the top layer of fabric 1/2"–1" away from quilting line with knot on top of fabric.

Some stitchers like to take a backstitch here at the beginning while others prefer to begin the first stitch here. Take small, even running stitches along the marked quilting line (Figure 15). Keep one hand positioned underneath to feel the needle go all the way through to the backing.

Figure 15
Make small, even running stitches on marked quilting line.

When you have nearly run out of thread, wind the thread around the needle several times to make a small knot and pull it close to the fabric. Insert the needle into the fabric on the quilting line and come out with the needle ½" to 1" away, pulling the knot into the fabric layers the same as when you started. Pull and cut thread close to fabric. The end should disappear inside after cutting. Some quilters prefer to take a backstitch with a loop through it for a knot to end.

Machine Quilting. Successful machine quilting requires practice and a good relationship with your sewing machine.

Prepare the quilt for machine quilting in the same way as for hand quilting. Use safety pins to hold the layers together instead of basting with thread.

Presser-foot quilting is best used for straight-line quilting because the presser bar lever does not need to be continually lifted.

Set the machine on a longer stitch length (3.0 or 8–10 stitches to the inch). Too tight a stitch causes puckering and fabric

General Instructions

tucks, either on the quilt top or backing. An even-feed or walking foot helps to eliminate the tucks and puckering by feeding the upper and lower layers through the machine evenly. Before you begin, loosen the amount of pressure on the presser foot.

Special machine-quilting needles work best to penetrate the three layers in your quilt.

Decide on a design. Quilting in the ditch is not quite as visible, but if you quilt with the feed dogs engaged, it means turning the quilt frequently. It is not easy to fit a rolled-up quilt through the small opening on the sewing machine head.

Meander quilting is the easiest way to machine-quilt—and it is fun. Meander quilting is done using an appliqué or darning foot with the feed dogs dropped. It is sort of like scribbling. Simply move the quilt top around under the foot and make stitches in a random pattern to fill the space. The same method may be used to outline a quilt design. The trick is the same as in hand quilting; you are striving for stitches of uniform size. Your hands are in complete control of the design.

If machine quilting is of interest to you, there are several very good books available at quilt shops that will help you become a successful machine quilter.

Finishing the Edges

After your quilt is tied or quilted, the edges need to be finished. Decide how you want the edges of your quilt finished before layering the backing and batting with the quilt top.

Without Binding—Self-Finish. There is one way to eliminate adding an edge finish. This is done before quilting. Place the batting on a flat surface. Place the pieced top right side up on the batting. Place the backing right sides together with the pieced top. Pin and/or baste the layers together to hold flat referring to Layering the Quilt Sandwich.

Begin stitching in the center of one side using a ¼" seam allowance, reversing at the beginning and end of the seam. Continue stitching all around and back to the beginning side. Leave a 12" or larger opening. Clip corners to reduce excess. Turn right side out through the opening. Slipstitch the opening closed by hand. The quilt may now be quilted by hand or machine.

The disadvantage to this method is that once the edges are sewn in, any creases or wrinkles that might form during the quilting process cannot be flattened out. Tying is the preferred method for finishing a quilt constructed using this method.

Bringing the backing fabric to the front is another way to finish the quilt's edge without binding. To accomplish this, complete the quilt as for hand or machine quilting. Trim the batting only even with the front. Trim the backing 1" larger than the completed top all around.

Turn the backing edge in ½" and then turn over to the front along edge of batting. The folded edge may be machine-stitched close to the edge through all layers, or blind-stitched in place to finish.

The front may be turned to the back. If using this method, a wider front border is needed. The backing and batting are trimmed 1" smaller than the top and the top edge is turned under ½" and then turned to the back and stitched in place.

One more method of self-finish may be used. The top and backing may be stitched together by hand at the edge. To accomplish this, all quilting must be stopped ½" from the quilt-top edge. The top and backing of the quilt are trimmed even and the batting is trimmed to ¼"–½" smaller. The edges of the top and backing are turned in ¼"–½" and blind-stitched together at the very edge.

These methods do not require the use of extra fabric and save time in preparation of binding strips; they are not as durable as an added binding.

Binding. The technique of adding extra fabric at the edges of the quilt is called binding. The binding encloses the edges and adds an extra layer of fabric for durability.

To prepare the quilt for the addition of the binding, trim the batting and backing layers flush with the top of the quilt using a rotary cutter and ruler or shears. Using a walking-foot attachment (sometimes called an even-feed foot attachment), machine-baste the three layers together all around approximately ⅛" from the cut edge.

The materials listed for each quilt in this book often includes a number of yards of self-made or purchased binding. Bias binding may be purchased in packages and in many colors. The advantage to self-made binding is that you can use fabrics from